HORDE™

MARGUERITE BENNETT
LEILA LEIZ

GUY MAJOR
MARSHALL DILLON

AFTERSHOCK™

MARGUERITE BENNETT co-creator & writer

LEILA LEIZ co-creator & artist

GUY MAJOR colorist

MARSHALL DILLON letterer

LEILA LEIZ cover & variant cover

CHARLES PRITCHETT book designer and production

DYLAN TODD logo designer

JOE PRUETT editor

AFTERSHOCK™

MIKE MARTS - Editor-in-Chief • JOE PRUETT - Publisher/Chief Creative Officer • LEE KRAMER - President • JON KRAMER - Chief Executive Officer
STEVE ROTTERDAM - SVP, Sales & Marketing • DAN SHIRES - VP, Film & Television UK • CHRISTINA HARRINGTON - Managing Editor
MARC HAMMOND - Sr. Retail Sales Development Manager • RUTHANN THOMPSON - Sr. Retailer Relations Manager • BLAKE STOCKER - Director of Finance
AARON MARION - Publicist • LISA MOODY - Finance • STEPHAN NILSON - Publishing Operations • JAWAD QURESHI - Technology Advisor / Strategist
RYAN CARROLL - Development Coordinator • CHARLES PRITCHETT - Comics Production • COREY BREEN - Collections Production
TEDDY LEO - Editorial Assistant • STEPHANIE CASEBIER & SARAH PRUETT - Publishing Assistants

AfterShock Logo Design by COMICRAFT
Publicity: contact AARON MARION (aaron@publichausagency.com) & RYAN CROY (ryan@publichausagency.com)
Special thanks to MARINE KSADZHIKYAN, IRA KURGAN, ANTONIA LIANOS & JULIE PIFHER

AFTERSHOCKCOMICS.COM Follow us on social media 🐦 📷 f

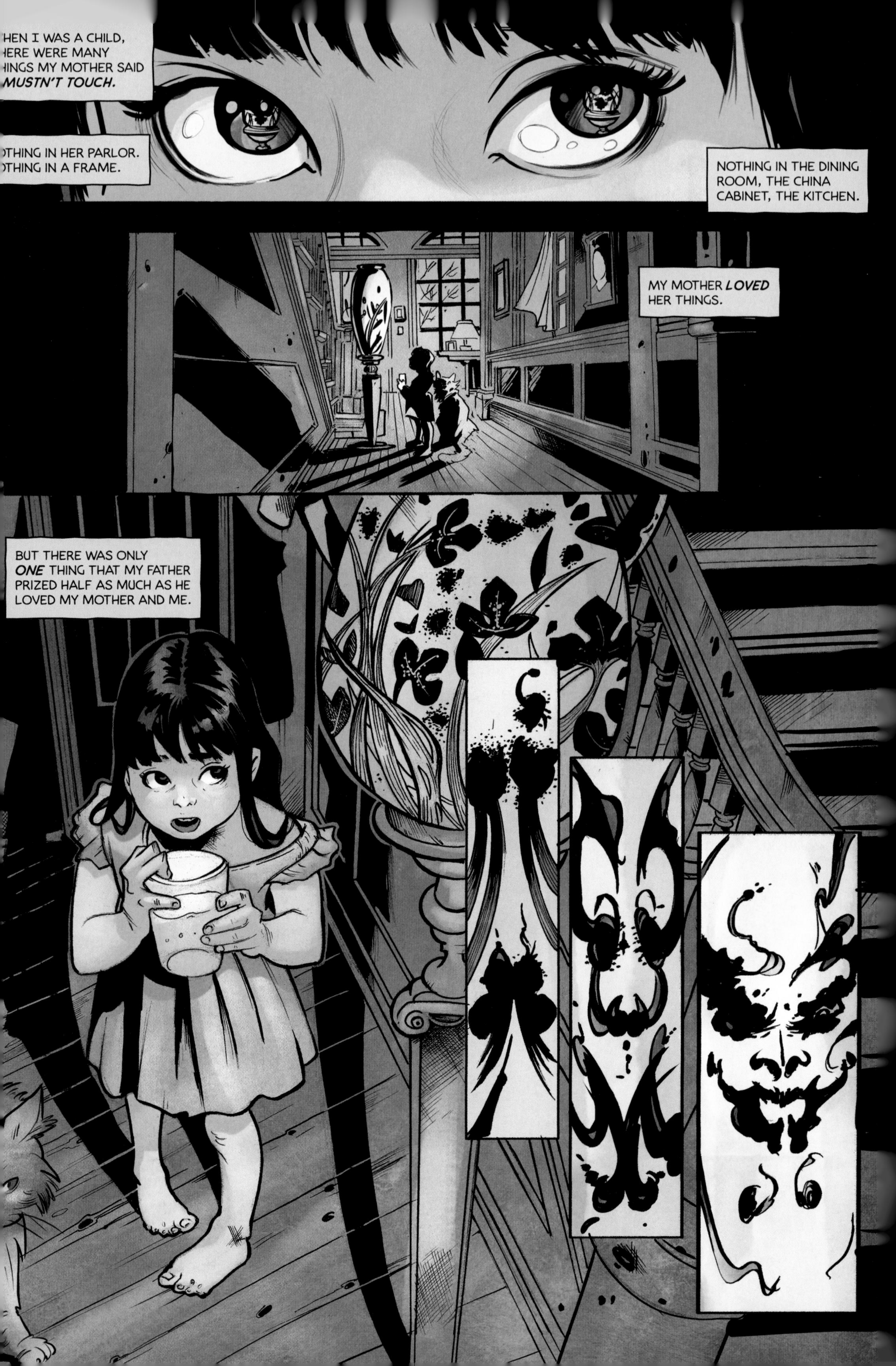
HEN I WAS A CHILD,
HERE WERE MANY
HINGS MY MOTHER SAID
MUSTN'T TOUCH.
OTHING IN HER PARLOR.
OTHING IN A FRAME.
NOTHING IN THE DINING ROOM, THE CHINA CABINET, THE KITCHEN.
MY MOTHER LOVED HER THINGS.
BUT THERE WAS ONLY ONE THING THAT MY FATHER PRIZED HALF AS MUCH AS HE LOVED MY MOTHER AND ME.

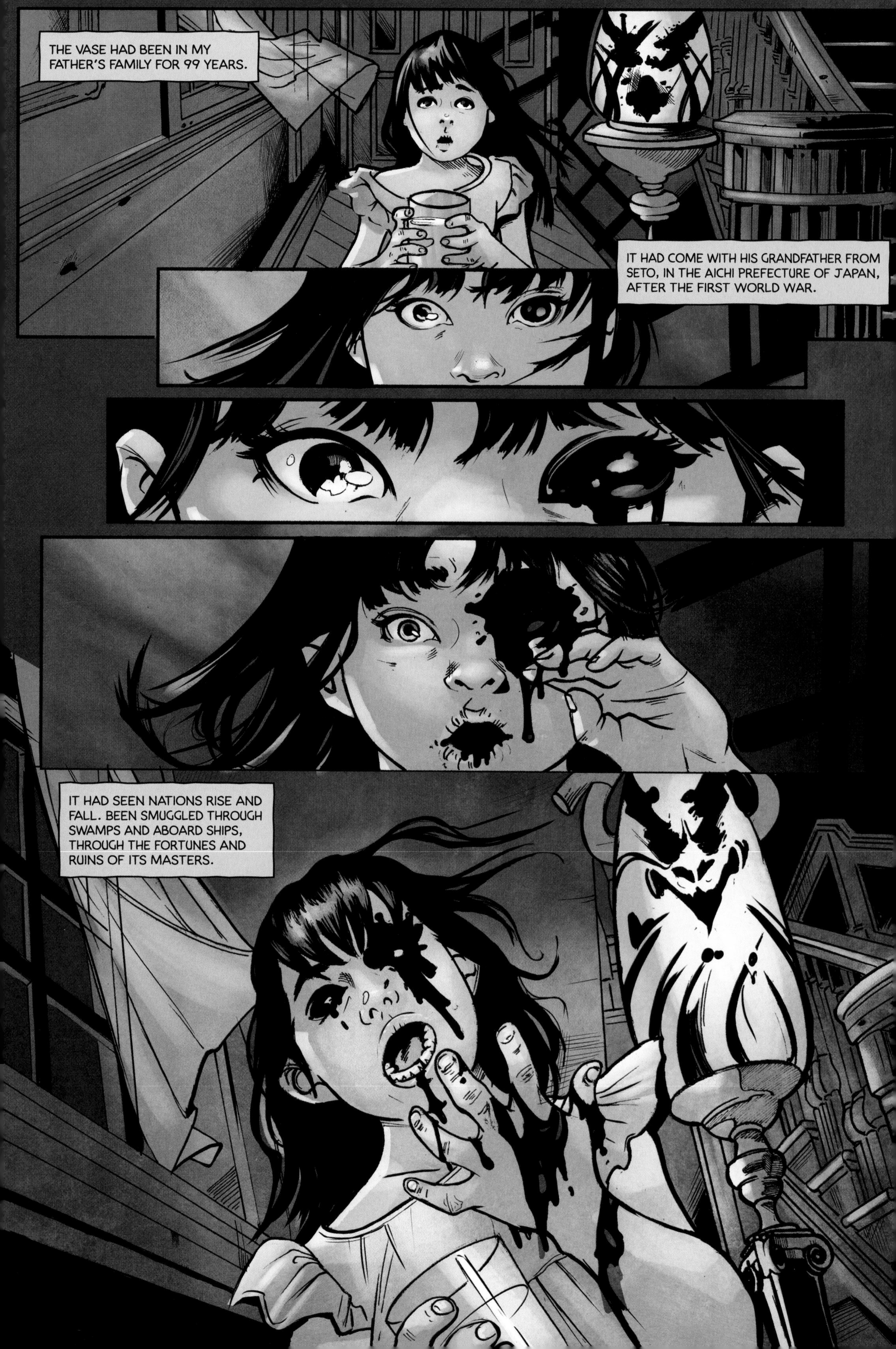
THE VASE HAD BEEN IN MY FATHER'S FAMILY FOR 99 YEARS.
IT HAD COME WITH HIS GRANDFATHER FROM SETO, IN THE AICHI PREFECTURE OF JAPAN, AFTER THE FIRST WORLD WAR.
IT HAD SEEN NATIONS RISE AND FALL. BEEN SMUGGLED THROUGH SWAMPS AND ABOARD SHIPS, THROUGH THE FORTUNES AND RUINS OF ITS MASTERS.

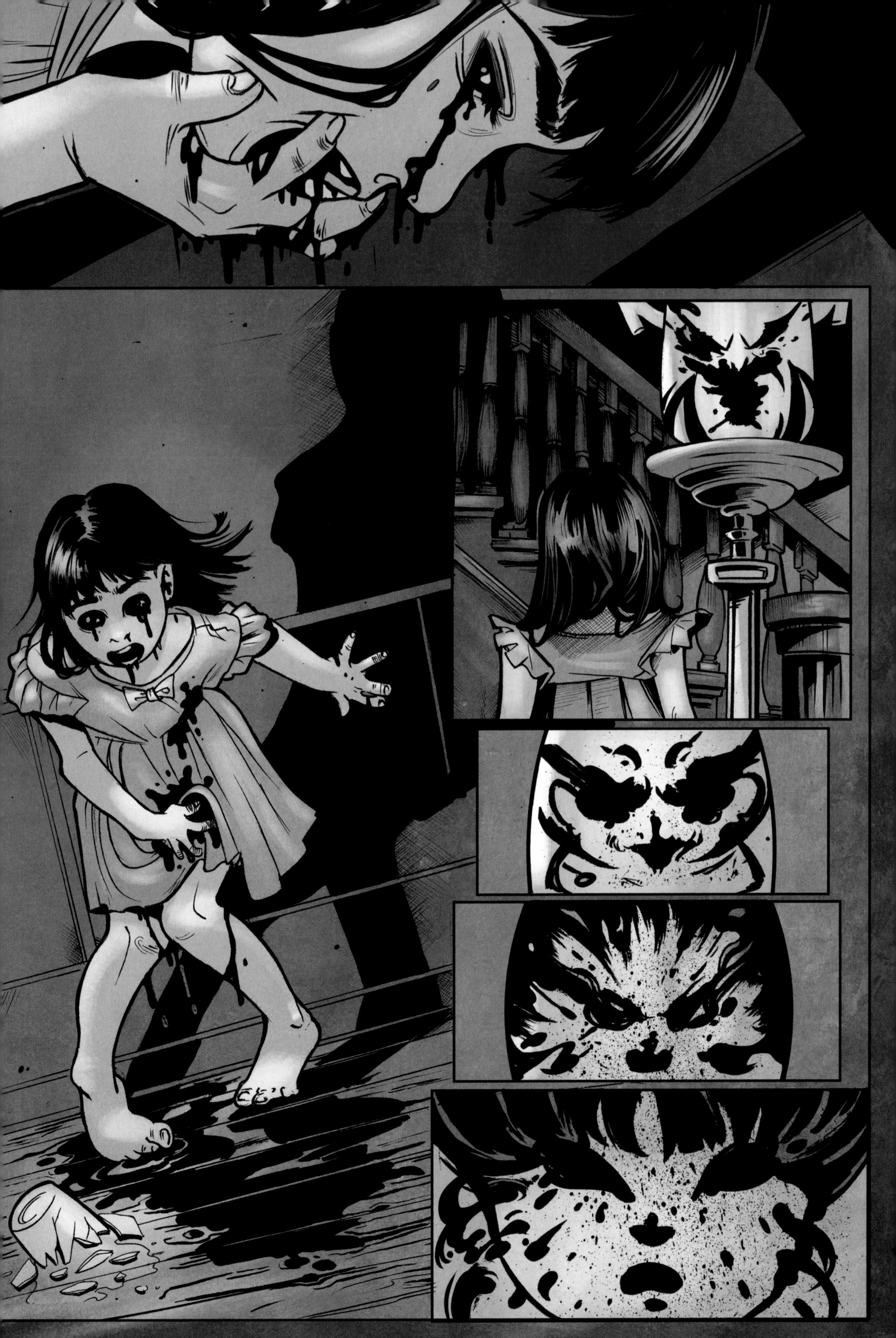

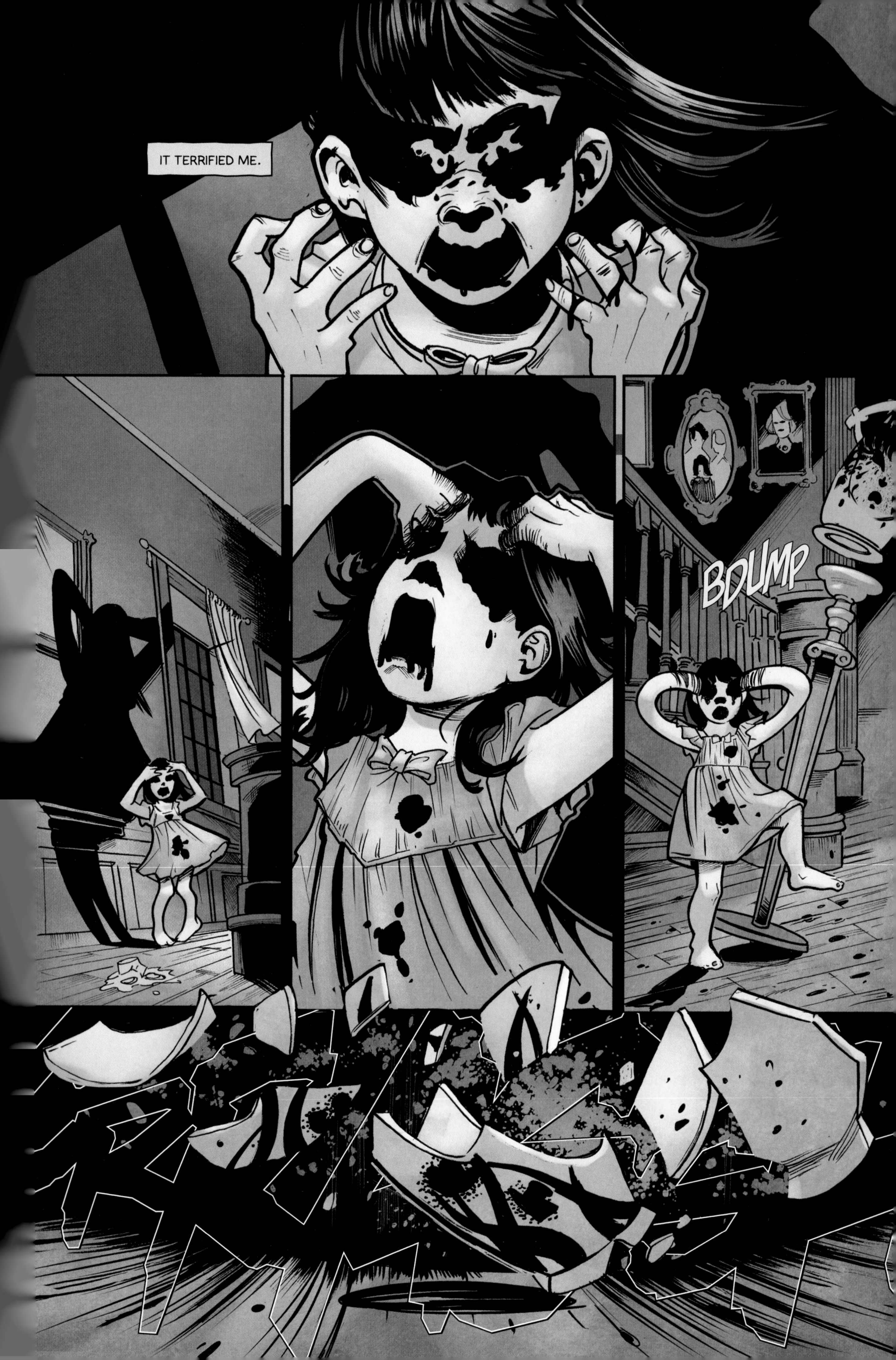
IT TERRIFIED ME.
BDUMP

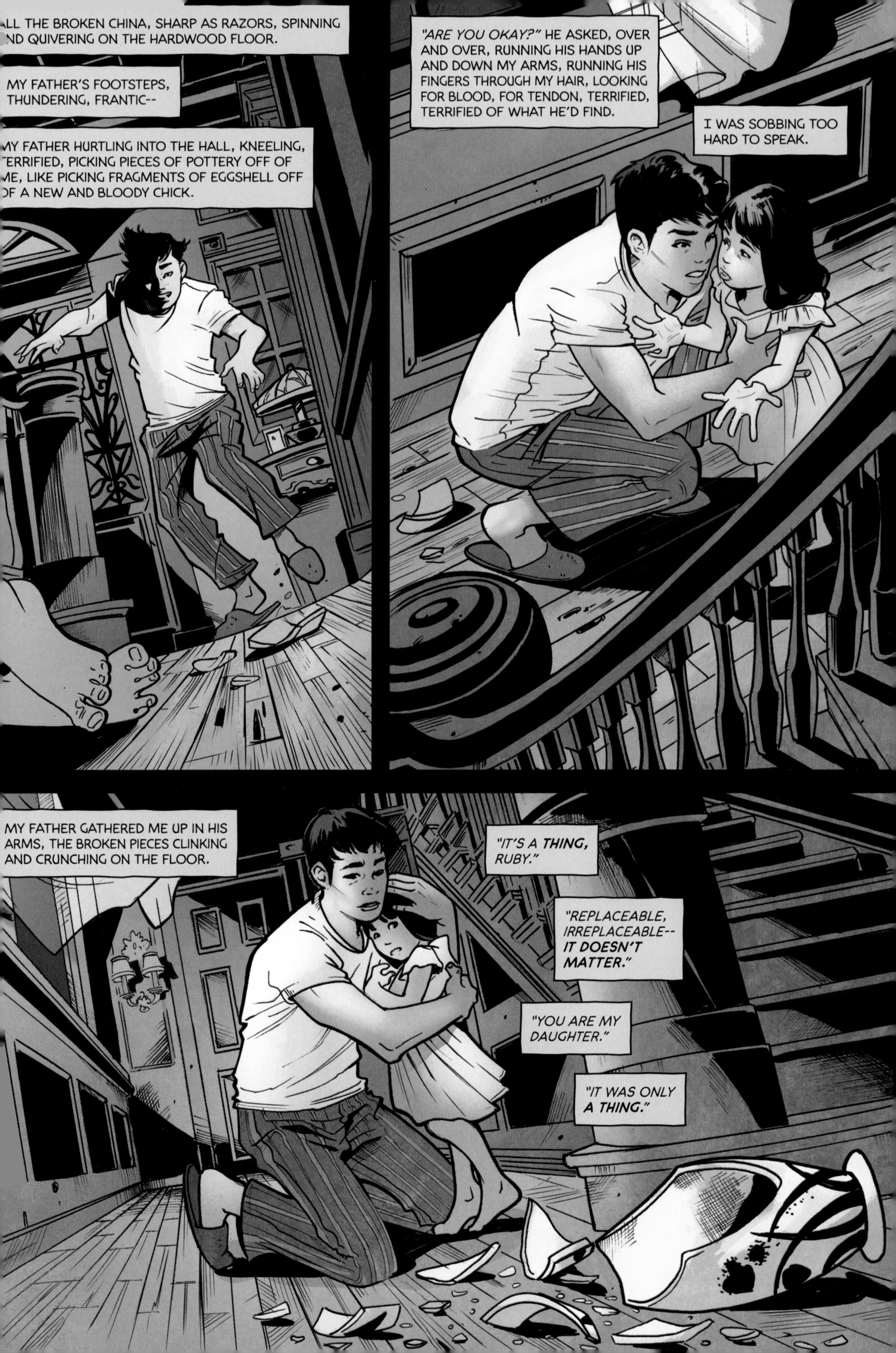

LL THE BROKEN CHINA, SHARP AS RAZORS, SPINNING
ND QUIVERING ON THE HARDWOOD FLOOR.
MY FATHER'S FOOTSTEPS, THUNDERING, FRANTIC--
MY FATHER HURTLING INTO THE HALL, KNEELING, ERRIFIED, PICKING PIECES OF POTTERY OFF OF ME, LIKE PICKING FRAGMENTS OF EGGSHELL OFF OF A NEW AND BLOODY CHICK.
"ARE YOU OKAY?" HE ASKED, OVER AND OVER, RUNNING HIS HANDS UP AND DOWN MY ARMS, RUNNING HIS FINGERS THROUGH MY HAIR, LOOKING FOR BLOOD, FOR TENDON, TERRIFIED, TERRIFIED OF WHAT HE'D FIND.
I WAS SOBBING TOO HARD TO SPEAK.
MY FATHER GATHERED ME UP IN HIS ARMS, THE BROKEN PIECES CLINKING AND CRUNCHING ON THE FLOOR.
"IT'S A THING, RUBY."
"REPLACEABLE, IRREPLACEABLE-- IT DOESN'T MATTER."
"YOU ARE MY DAUGHTER."
"IT WAS ONLY A THING."

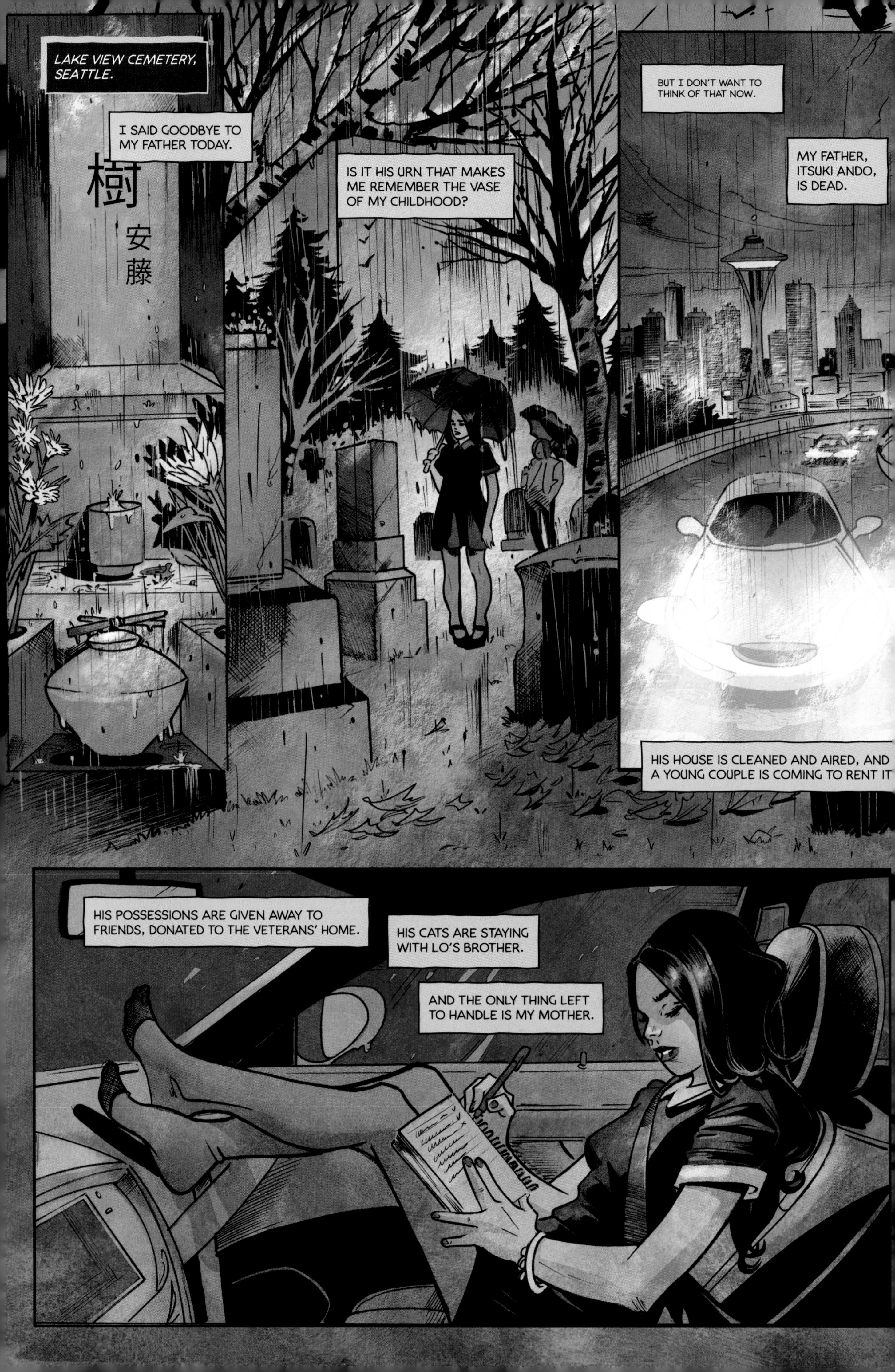
LAKE VIEW CEMETERY, SEATTLE.
I SAID GOODBYE TO MY FATHER TODAY.
樹
安藤
IS IT HIS URN THAT MAKES ME REMEMBER THE VASE OF MY CHILDHOOD?
BUT I DON'T WANT TO THINK OF THAT NOW.
MY FATHER, ITSUKI ANDO, IS DEAD.
HIS HOUSE IS CLEANED AND AIRED, AND A YOUNG COUPLE IS COMING TO RENT IT
HIS POSSESSIONS ARE GIVEN AWAY TO FRIENDS, DONATED TO THE VETERANS' HOME.
HIS CATS ARE STAYING WITH LO'S BROTHER.
AND THE ONLY THING LEFT TO HANDLE IS MY MOTHER.

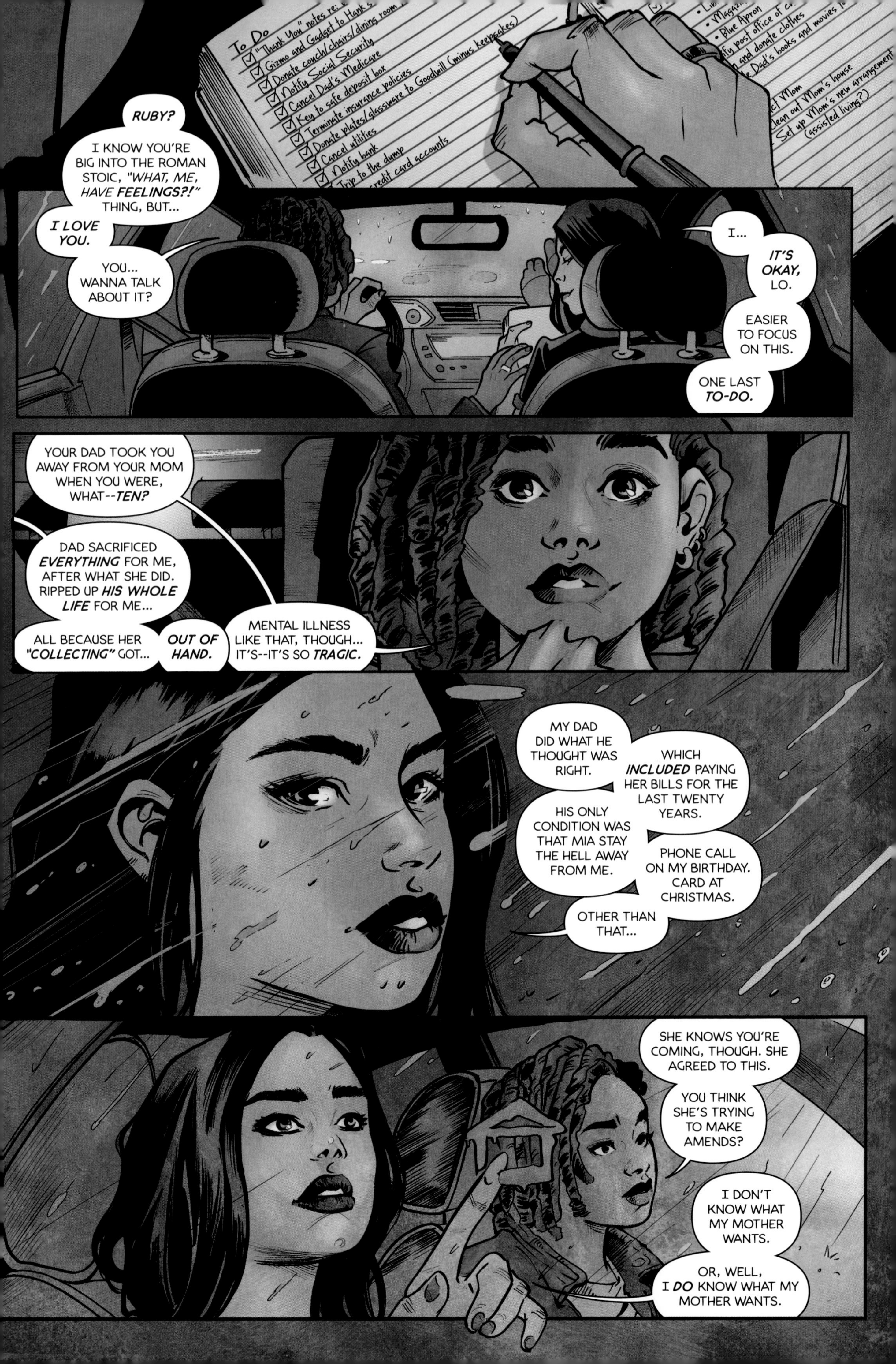
To Do
"Thank You" notes re:
Gizmo and Gadget to Hank's
Donate couch/chairs/dining room
Notify Social Security
Cancel Dad's Medicare
Key to safe deposit box
Terminate insurance policies
Donate plates/glassware to Goodwill (minus keepsakes)
Donate utilities
Cancel utilities
Notify bank
Trip to the dump
credit card accounts
• Blue Apron
and donate clothes
Dad's books and movies
Clean out Mom's house
Set up Mom's new arrangement
(assisted living?)
RUBY?
I KNOW YOU'RE BIG INTO THE ROMAN STOIC, "WHAT, ME, HAVE FEELINGS?!" THING, BUT...
I LOVE YOU.
YOU... WANNA TALK ABOUT IT?
I...
IT'S OKAY, LO.
EASIER TO FOCUS ON THIS.
ONE LAST TO-DO.
YOUR DAD TOOK YOU AWAY FROM YOUR MOM WHEN YOU WERE, WHAT--TEN?
DAD SACRIFICED EVERYTHING FOR ME, AFTER WHAT SHE DID. RIPPED UP HIS WHOLE LIFE FOR ME...
ALL BECAUSE HER "COLLECTING" GOT...
OUT OF HAND.
MENTAL ILLNESS LIKE THAT, THOUGH... IT'S--IT'S SO TRAGIC.
MY DAD DID WHAT HE THOUGHT WAS RIGHT.
WHICH INCLUDED PAYING HER BILLS FOR THE LAST TWENTY YEARS.
HIS ONLY CONDITION WAS THAT MIA STAY THE HELL AWAY FROM ME.
PHONE CALL ON MY BIRTHDAY. CARD AT CHRISTMAS.
OTHER THAN THAT...
SHE KNOWS YOU'RE COMING, THOUGH. SHE AGREED TO THIS.
YOU THINK SHE'S TRYING TO MAKE AMENDS?
I DON'T KNOW WHAT MY MOTHER WANTS.
OR, WELL, I DO KNOW WHAT MY MOTHER WANTS.

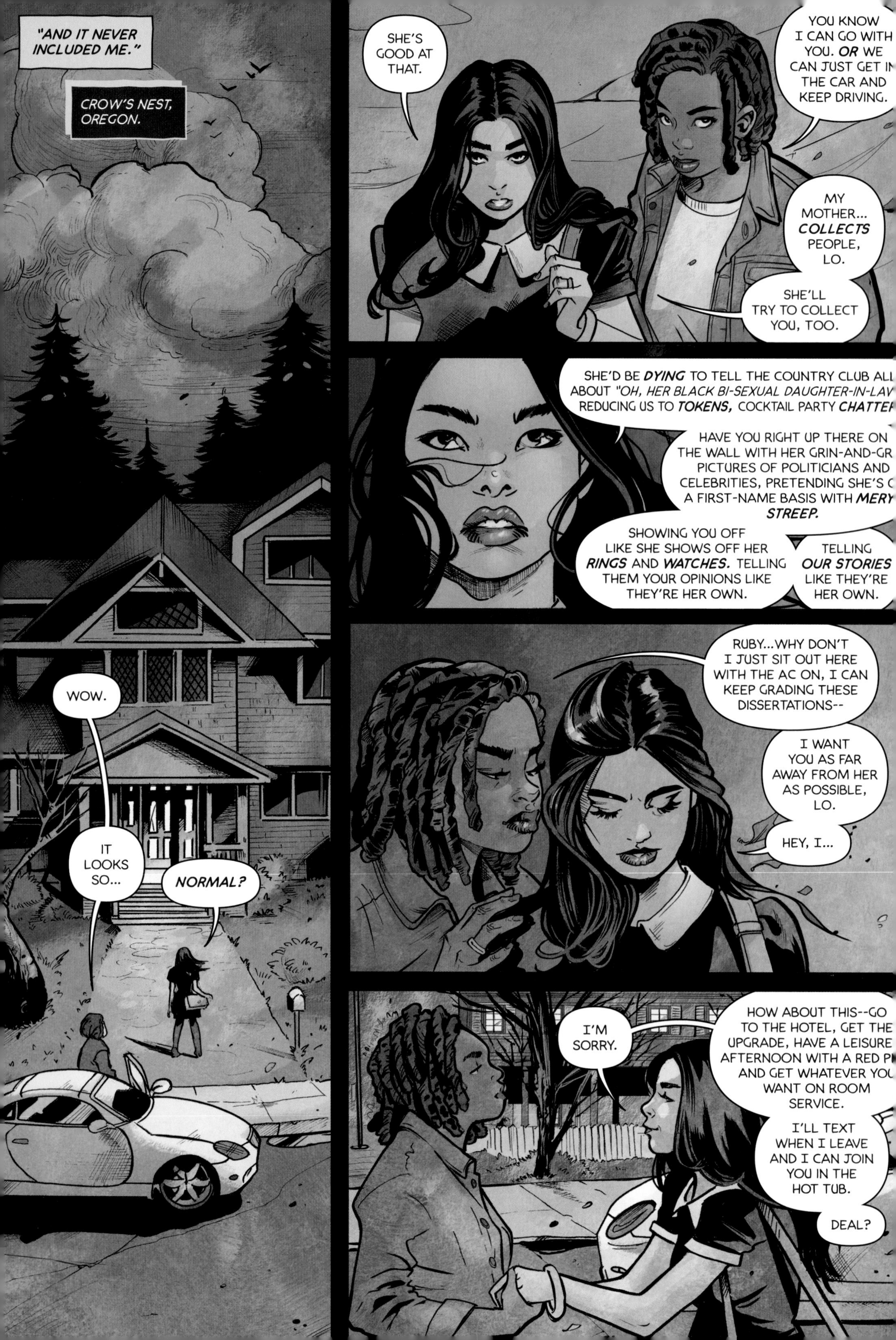
"AND IT NEVER INCLUDED ME."
CROW'S NEST, OREGON.
WOW.
IT LOOKS SO...
NORMAL?
SHE'S GOOD AT THAT.
YOU KNOW I CAN GO WITH YOU. OR WE CAN JUST GET IN THE CAR AND KEEP DRIVING.
MY MOTHER... COLLECTS PEOPLE, LO.
SHE'LL TRY TO COLLECT YOU, TOO.
SHE'D BE DYING TO TELL THE COUNTRY CLUB ALL ABOUT "OH, HER BLACK BI-SEXUAL DAUGHTER-IN-LAW" REDUCING US TO TOKENS, COCKTAIL PARTY CHATTER.
HAVE YOU RIGHT UP THERE ON THE WALL WITH HER GRIN-AND-GR PICTURES OF POLITICIANS AND CELEBRITIES, PRETENDING SHE'S ON A FIRST-NAME BASIS WITH MERYL STREEP.
SHOWING YOU OFF LIKE SHE SHOWS OFF HER RINGS AND WATCHES. TELLING THEM YOUR OPINIONS LIKE THEY'RE HER OWN.
TELLING OUR STORIES LIKE THEY'RE HER OWN.
RUBY...WHY DON'T I JUST SIT OUT HERE WITH THE AC ON, I CAN KEEP GRADING THESE DISSERTATIONS--
I WANT YOU AS FAR AWAY FROM HER AS POSSIBLE, LO.
HEY, I...
I'M SORRY.
HOW ABOUT THIS--GO TO THE HOTEL, GET THE UPGRADE, HAVE A LEISURE AFTERNOON WITH A RED P AND GET WHATEVER YOU WANT ON ROOM SERVICE.
I'LL TEXT WHEN I LEAVE AND I CAN JOIN YOU IN THE HOT TUB.
DEAL?

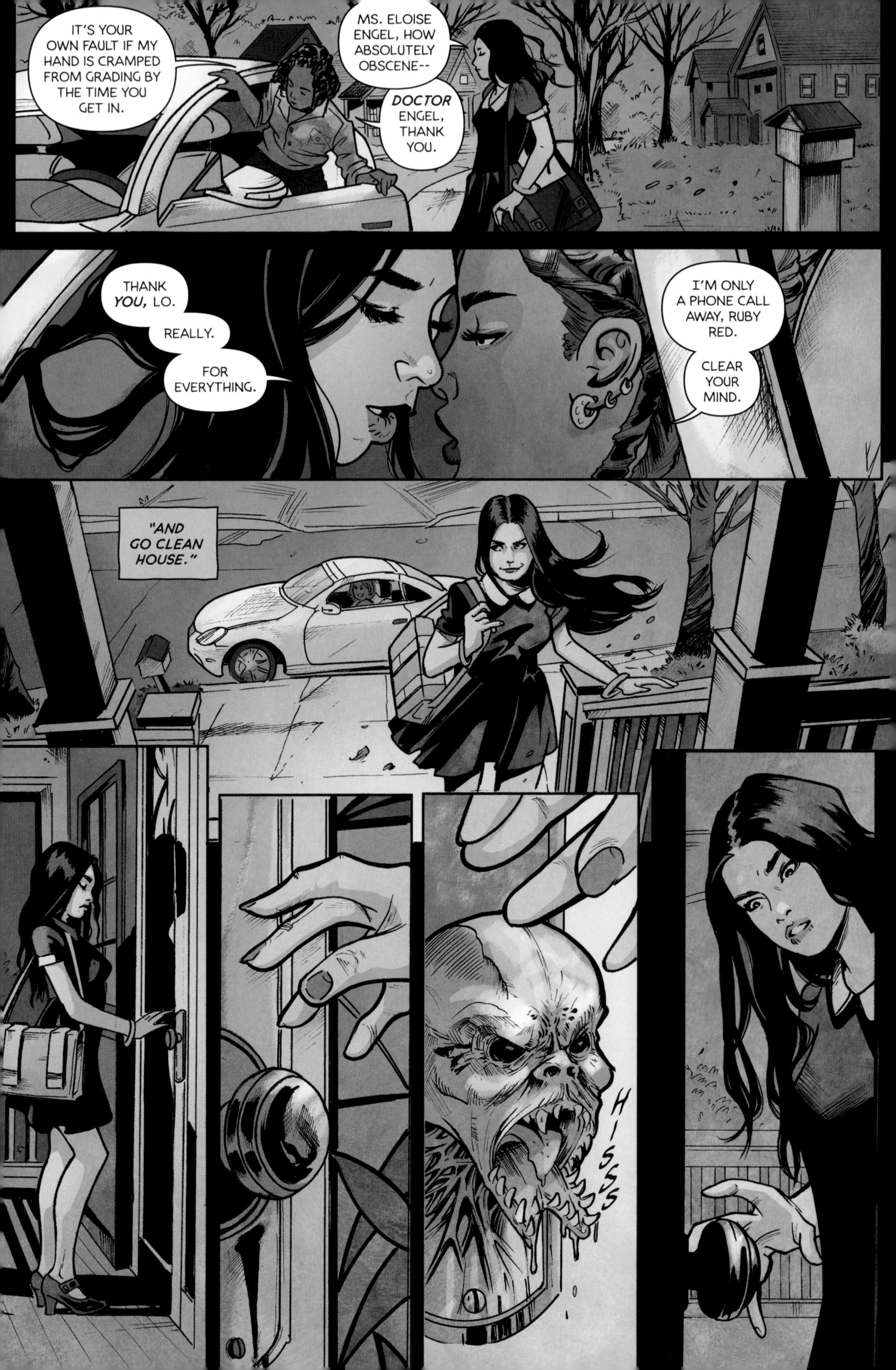
IT'S YOUR OWN FAULT IF MY HAND IS CRAMPED FROM GRADING BY THE TIME YOU GET IN.
MS. ELOISE ENGEL, HOW ABSOLUTELY OBSCENE--
DOCTOR ENGEL, THANK YOU.
THANK YOU, LO.
REALLY.
FOR EVERYTHING.
I'M ONLY A PHONE CALL AWAY, RUBY RED.
CLEAR YOUR MIND.
"AND GO CLEAN HOUSE."
HISSS

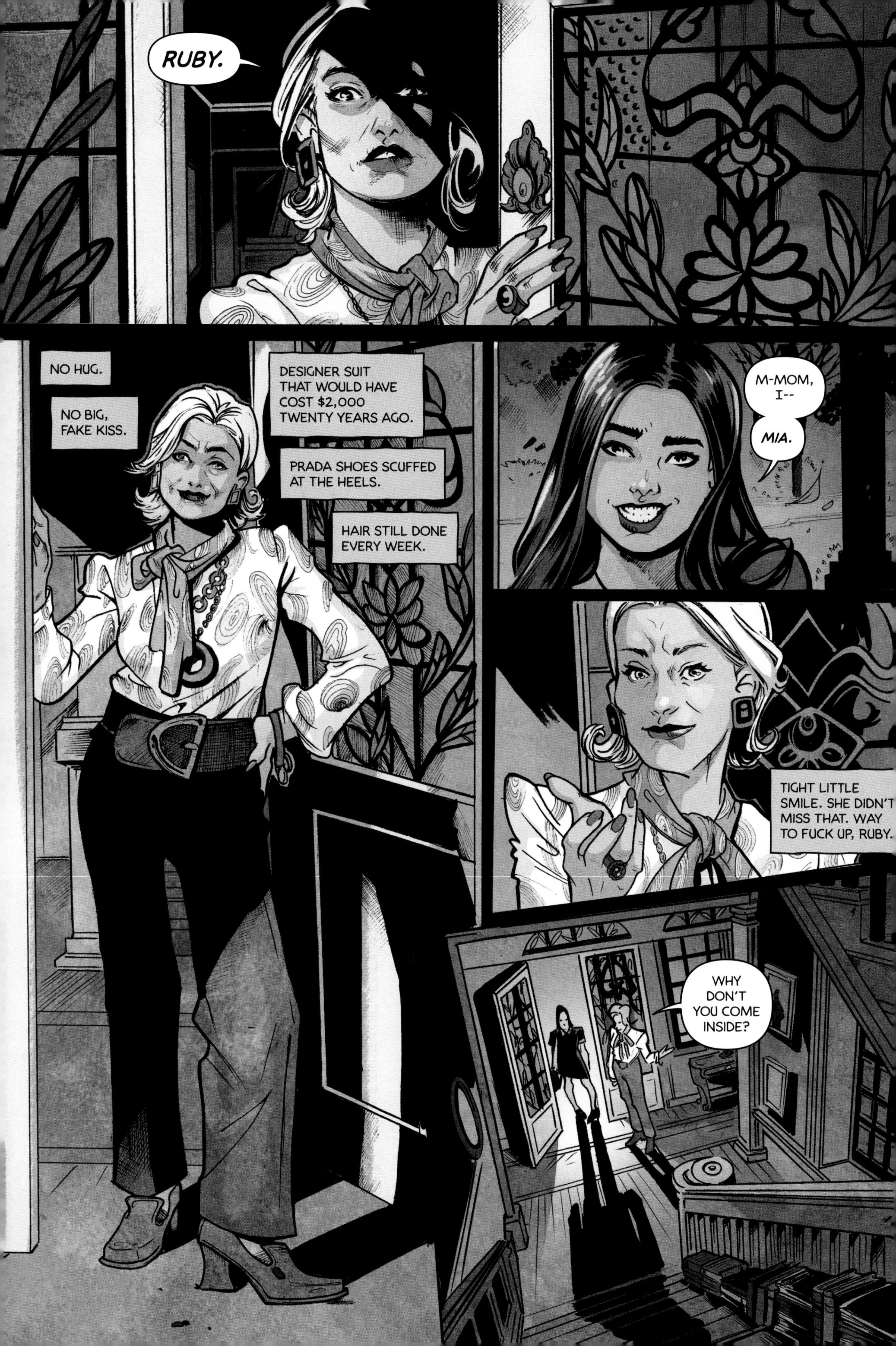
RUBY.
NO HUG.
NO BIG, FAKE KISS.
DESIGNER SUIT THAT WOULD HAVE COST $2,000 TWENTY YEARS AGO.
PRADA SHOES SCUFFED AT THE HEELS.
HAIR STILL DONE EVERY WEEK.
M-MOM, I--
MIA.
TIGHT LITTLE SMILE. SHE DIDN'T MISS THAT. WAY TO FUCK UP, RUBY.
WHY DON'T YOU COME INSIDE?

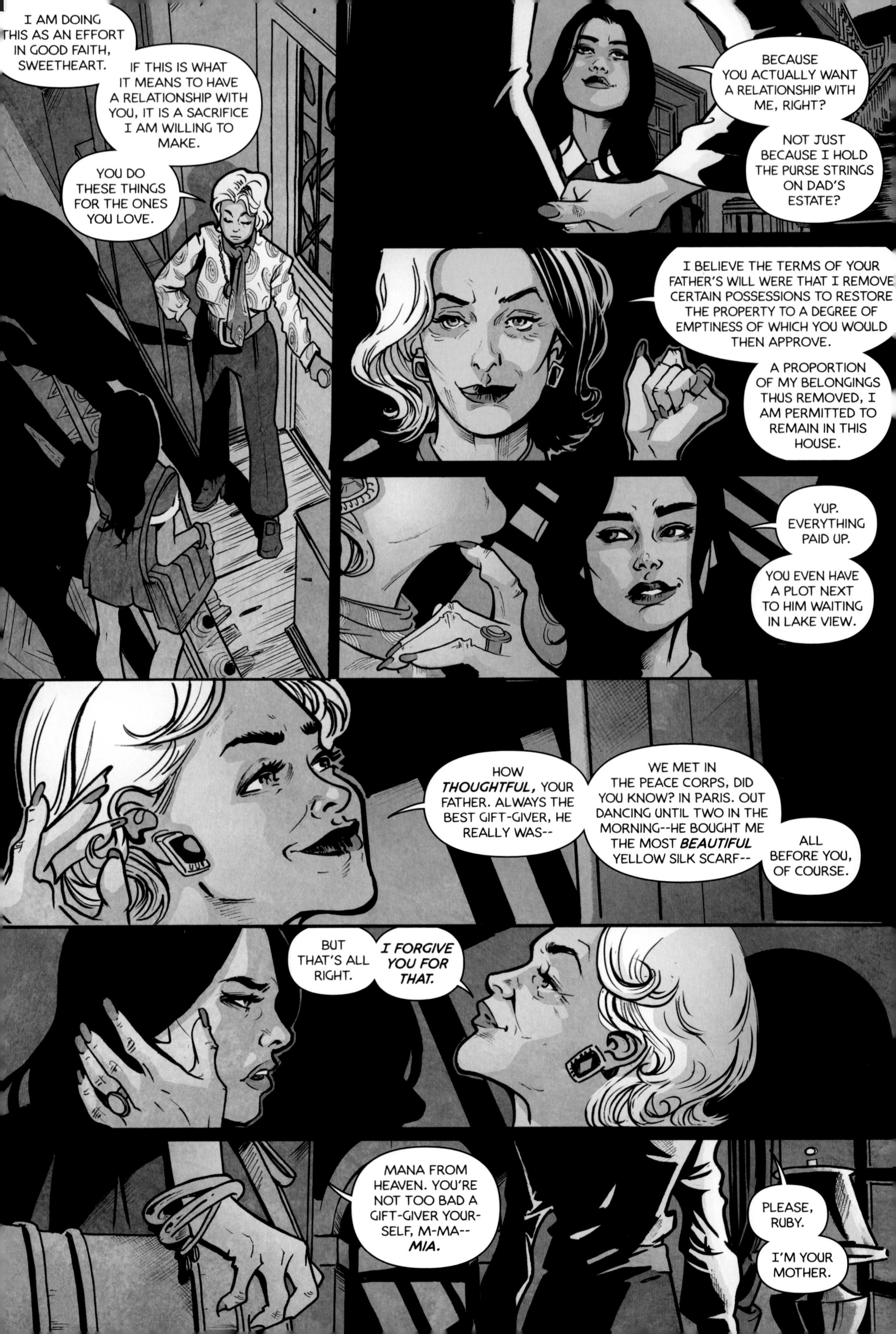
I AM DOING THIS AS AN EFFORT IN GOOD FAITH, SWEETHEART.
IF THIS IS WHAT IT MEANS TO HAVE A RELATIONSHIP WITH YOU, IT IS A SACRIFICE I AM WILLING TO MAKE.
YOU DO THESE THINGS FOR THE ONES YOU LOVE.
BECAUSE YOU ACTUALLY WANT A RELATIONSHIP WITH ME, RIGHT?
NOT JUST BECAUSE I HOLD THE PURSE STRINGS ON DAD'S ESTATE?
I BELIEVE THE TERMS OF YOUR FATHER'S WILL WERE THAT I REMOVE CERTAIN POSSESSIONS TO RESTORE THE PROPERTY TO A DEGREE OF EMPTINESS OF WHICH YOU WOULD THEN APPROVE.
A PROPORTION OF MY BELONGINGS THUS REMOVED, I AM PERMITTED TO REMAIN IN THIS HOUSE.
YUP. EVERYTHING PAID UP.
YOU EVEN HAVE A PLOT NEXT TO HIM WAITING IN LAKE VIEW.
HOW *THOUGHTFUL,* YOUR FATHER. ALWAYS THE BEST GIFT-GIVER, HE REALLY WAS--
WE MET IN THE PEACE CORPS, DID YOU KNOW? IN PARIS. OUT DANCING UNTIL TWO IN THE MORNING--HE BOUGHT ME THE MOST *BEAUTIFUL* YELLOW SILK SCARF--
ALL BEFORE YOU, OF COURSE.
BUT THAT'S ALL RIGHT.
I FORGIVE YOU FOR THAT.
MANA FROM HEAVEN. YOU'RE NOT TOO BAD A GIFT-GIVER YOURSELF, M-MA-- *MIA.*
PLEASE, RUBY.
I'M YOUR MOTHER.

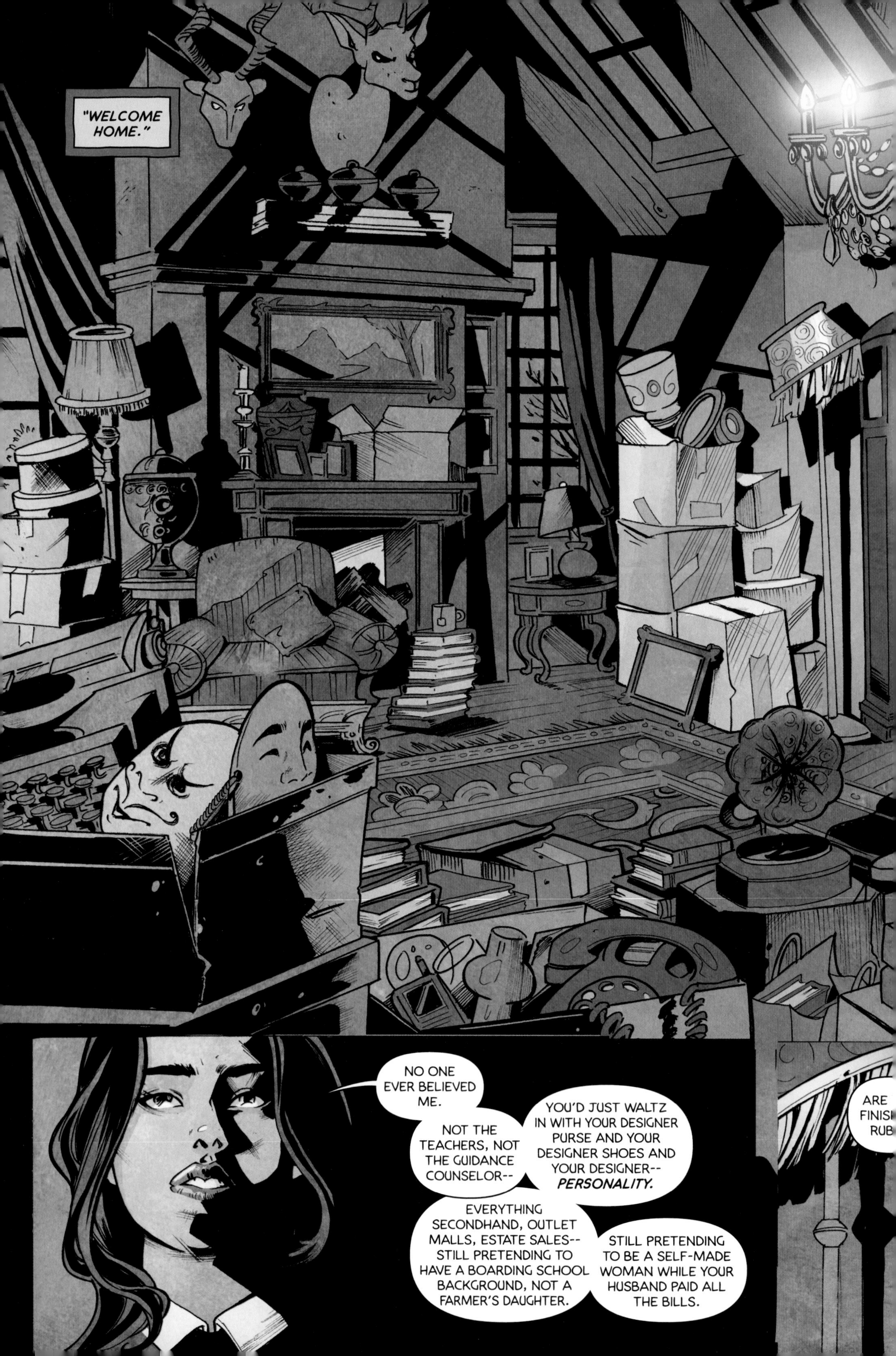
"WELCOME HOME."
NO ONE EVER BELIEVED ME.
NOT THE TEACHERS, NOT THE GUIDANCE COUNSELOR--
YOU'D JUST WALTZ IN WITH YOUR DESIGNER PURSE AND YOUR DESIGNER SHOES AND YOUR DESIGNER-- *PERSONALITY.*
EVERYTHING SECONDHAND, OUTLET MALLS, ESTATE SALES-- STILL PRETENDING TO HAVE A BOARDING SCHOOL BACKGROUND, NOT A FARMER'S DAUGHTER.
STILL PRETENDING TO BE A SELF-MADE WOMAN WHILE YOUR HUSBAND PAID ALL THE BILLS.
ARE

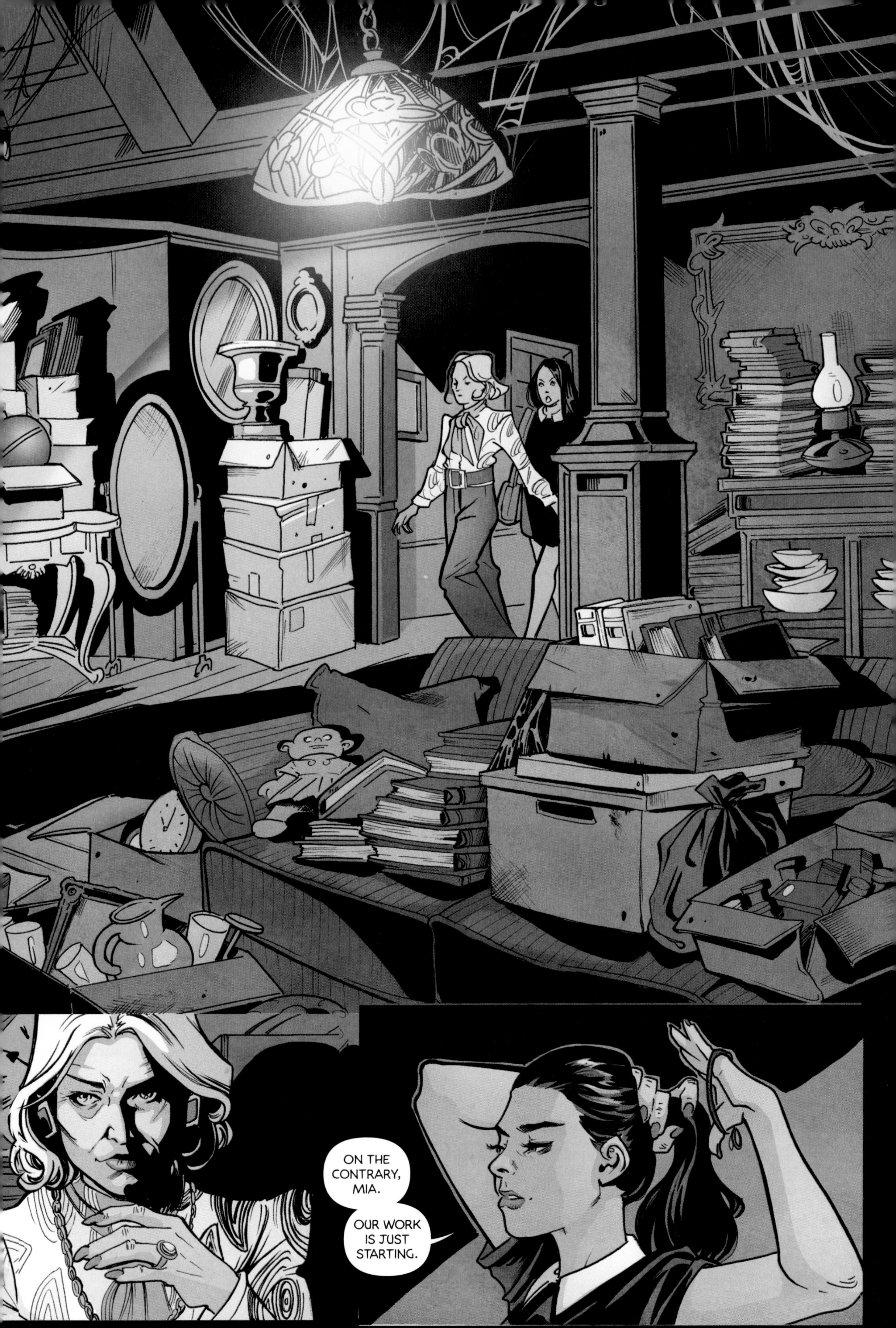

ON THE CONTRARY, MIA.
OUR WORK IS JUST STARTING.

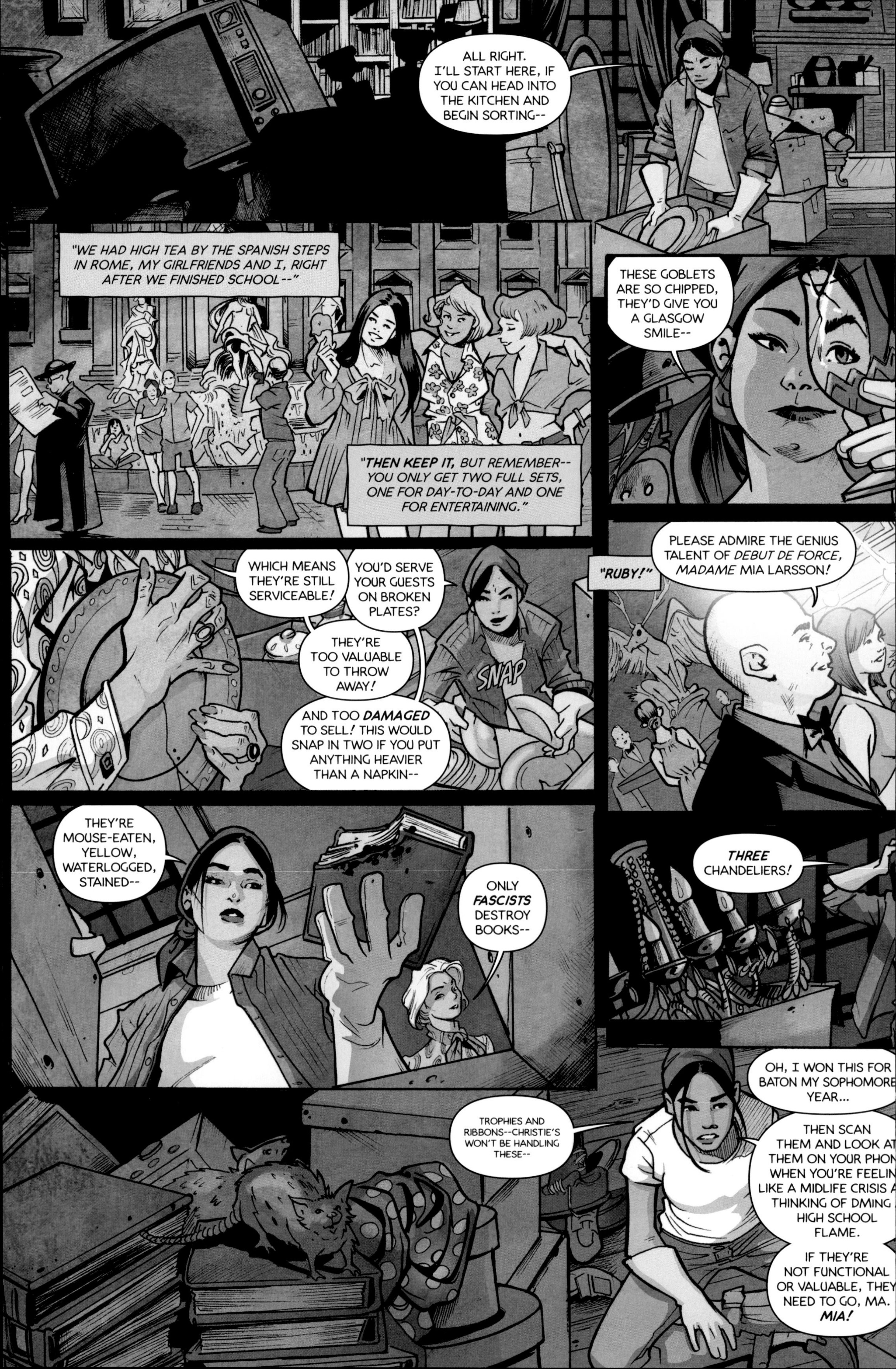
ALL RIGHT. I'LL START HERE, IF YOU CAN HEAD INTO THE KITCHEN AND BEGIN SORTING--
"WE HAD HIGH TEA BY THE SPANISH STEPS IN ROME, MY GIRLFRIENDS AND I, RIGHT AFTER WE FINISHED SCHOOL--"
"THEN KEEP IT, BUT REMEMBER-- YOU ONLY GET TWO FULL SETS, ONE FOR DAY-TO-DAY AND ONE FOR ENTERTAINING."
THESE GOBLETS ARE SO CHIPPED, THEY'D GIVE YOU A GLASGOW SMILE--
WHICH MEANS THEY'RE STILL SERVICEABLE!
YOU'D SERVE YOUR GUESTS ON BROKEN PLATES?
THEY'RE TOO VALUABLE TO THROW AWAY!
AND TOO DAMAGED TO SELL! THIS WOULD SNAP IN TWO IF YOU PUT ANYTHING HEAVIER THAN A NAPKIN--
SNAP
"RUBY!"
PLEASE ADMIRE THE GENIUS TALENT OF DEBUT DE FORCE, MADAME MIA LARSSON!
THEY'RE MOUSE-EATEN, YELLOW, WATERLOGGED, STAINED--
ONLY FASCISTS DESTROY BOOKS--
THREE CHANDELIERS!
TROPHIES AND RIBBONS--CHRISTIE'S WON'T BE HANDLING THESE--
OH, I WON THIS FOR BATON MY SOPHOMORE YEAR...
THEN SCAN THEM AND LOOK AT THEM ON YOUR PHON WHEN YOU'RE FEELIN LIKE A MIDLIFE CRISIS A THINKING OF DMING A HIGH SCHOOL FLAME.
IF THEY'RE NOT FUNCTIONAL OR VALUABLE, THEY NEED TO GO, MA. MIA!

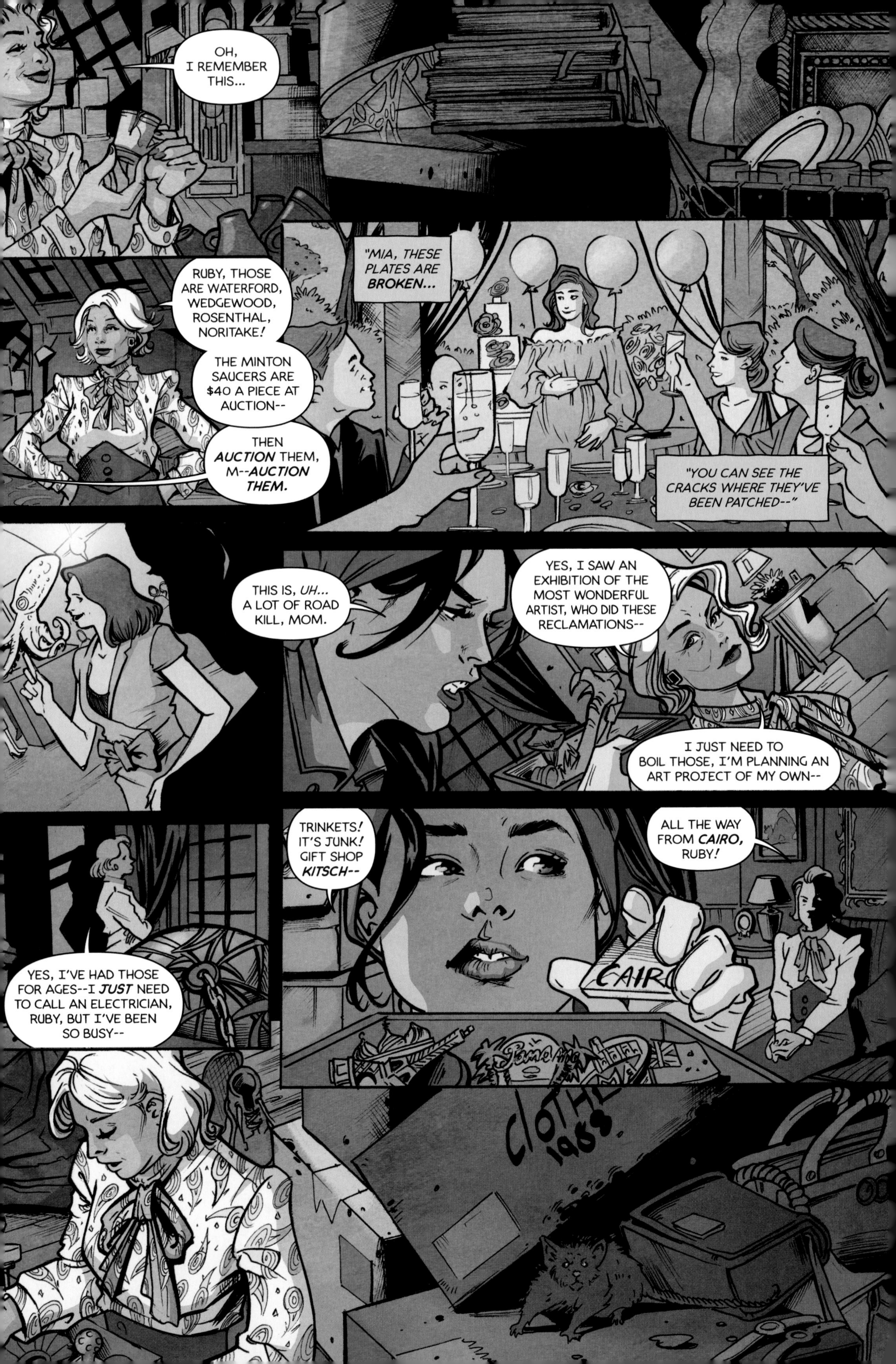
OH, I REMEMBER THIS...
"MIA, THESE PLATES ARE BROKEN...
RUBY, THOSE ARE WATERFORD, WEDGEWOOD, ROSENTHAL, NORITAKE!
THE MINTON SAUCERS ARE $40 A PIECE AT AUCTION--
THEN AUCTION THEM, M--AUCTION THEM.
"YOU CAN SEE THE CRACKS WHERE THEY'VE BEEN PATCHED--"
THIS IS, UH... A LOT OF ROAD KILL, MOM.
YES, I SAW AN EXHIBITION OF THE MOST WONDERFUL ARTIST, WHO DID THESE RECLAMATIONS--
I JUST NEED TO BOIL THOSE, I'M PLANNING AN ART PROJECT OF MY OWN--
TRINKETS! IT'S JUNK! GIFT SHOP KITSCH--
ALL THE WAY FROM CAIRO, RUBY!
CAIRO
YES, I'VE HAD THOSE FOR AGES--I JUST NEED TO CALL AN ELECTRICIAN, RUBY, BUT I'VE BEEN SO BUSY--
CLOTHES 1968

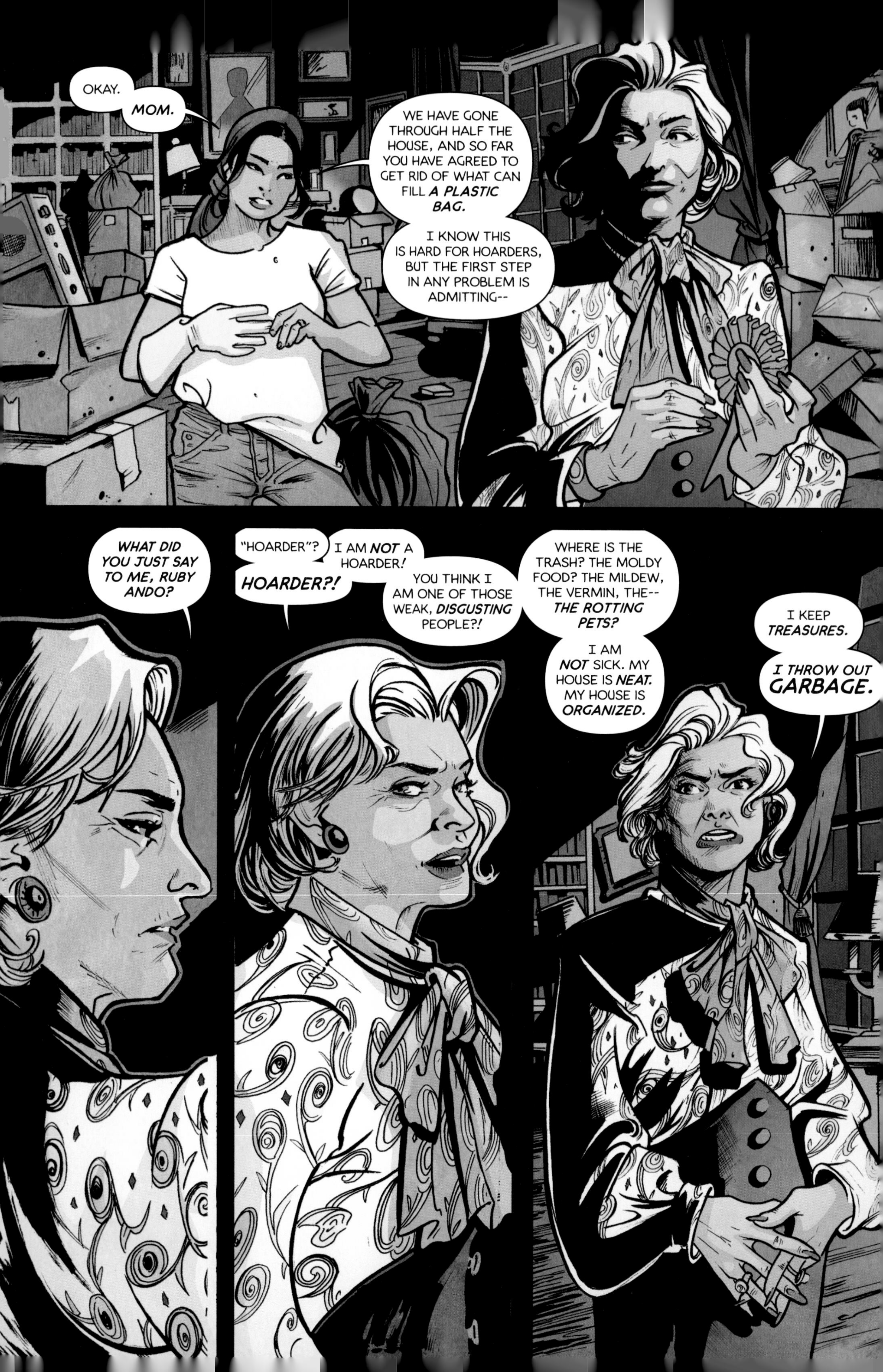
OKAY.
MOM.
WE HAVE GONE THROUGH HALF THE HOUSE, AND SO FAR YOU HAVE AGREED TO GET RID OF WHAT CAN FILL ***A PLASTIC BAG.***
I KNOW THIS IS HARD FOR HOARDERS, BUT THE FIRST STEP IN ANY PROBLEM IS ADMITTING--
WHAT DID YOU JUST SAY TO ME, RUBY ANDO?
"HOARDER"?
HOARDER?!
I AM ***NOT*** A HOARDER*!*
YOU THINK I AM ONE OF THOSE WEAK, ***DISGUSTING*** PEOPLE?*!*
WHERE IS THE TRASH? THE MOLDY FOOD? THE MILDEW, THE VERMIN, THE-- ***THE ROTTING PETS?***
I AM ***NOT*** SICK. MY HOUSE IS ***NEAT.*** MY HOUSE IS ***ORGANIZED.***
I KEEP ***TREASURES.***
I THROW OUT GARBAGE.

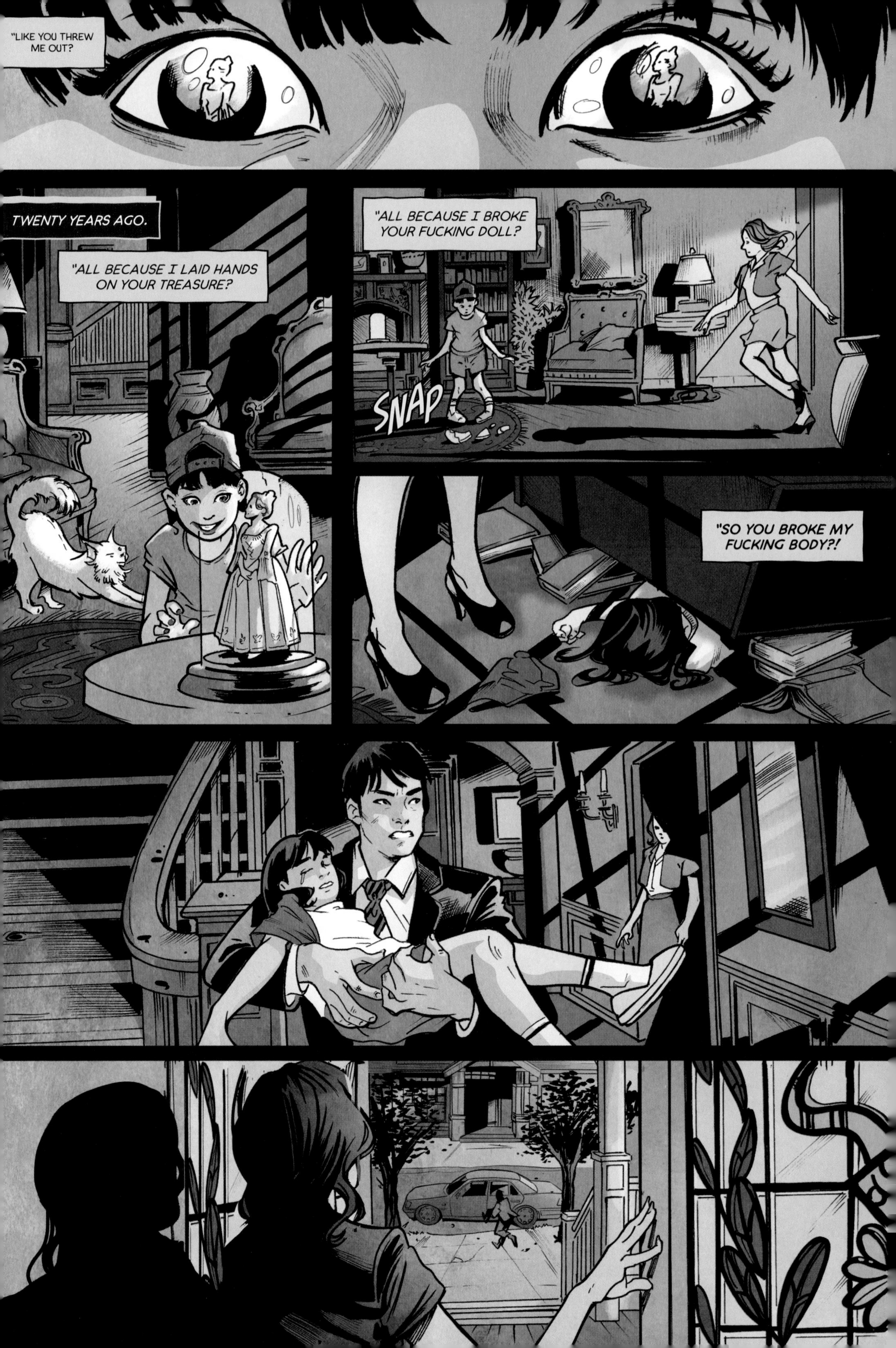
"LIKE YOU THREW ME OUT?
TWENTY YEARS AGO.
"ALL BECAUSE I LAID HANDS ON YOUR TREASURE?
"ALL BECAUSE I BROKE YOUR FUCKING DOLL?
SNAP
"SO YOU BROKE MY FUCKING BODY?!

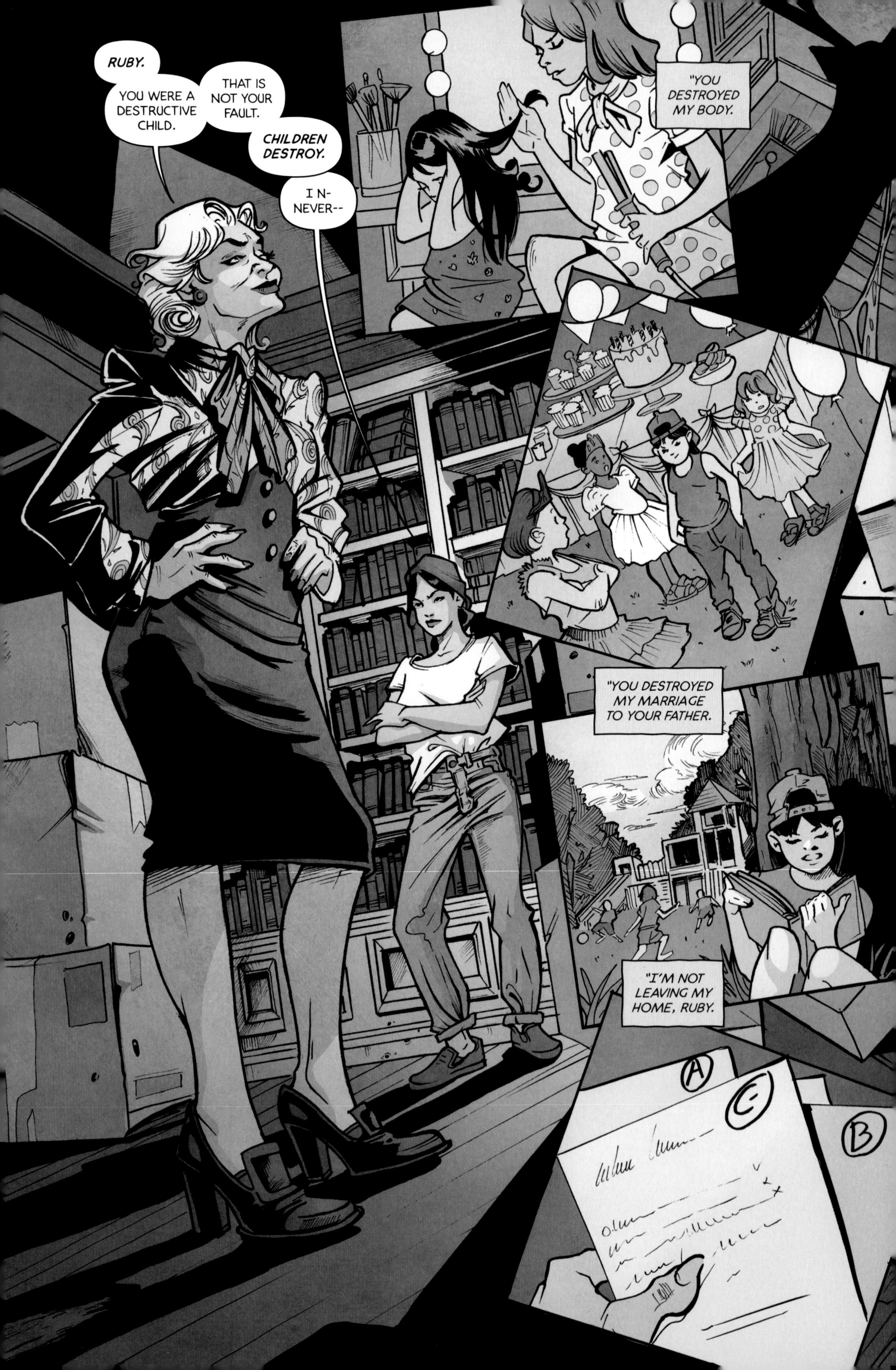
RUBY.
YOU WERE A DESTRUCTIVE CHILD.
THAT IS NOT YOUR FAULT.
CHILDREN DESTROY.
I N- NEVER--
"YOU DESTROYED MY BODY.
"YOU DESTROYED MY MARRIAGE TO YOUR FATHER.
"I'M NOT LEAVING MY HOME, RUBY.
A
C-
B

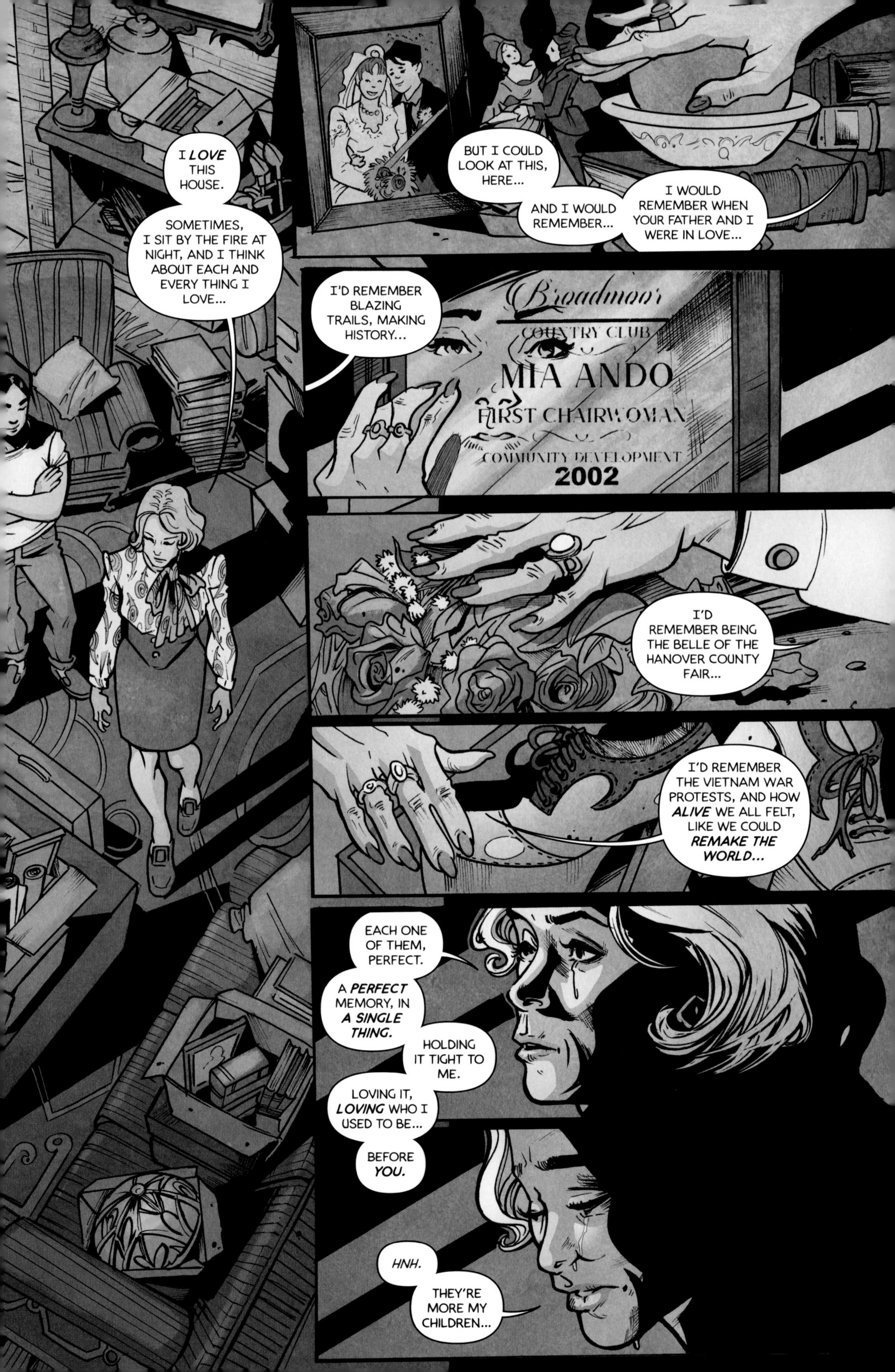
I LOVE THIS HOUSE.
SOMETIMES, I SIT BY THE FIRE AT NIGHT, AND I THINK ABOUT EACH AND EVERY THING I LOVE...
BUT I COULD LOOK AT THIS, HERE...
AND I WOULD REMEMBER...
I WOULD REMEMBER WHEN YOUR FATHER AND I WERE IN LOVE...
I'D REMEMBER BLAZING TRAILS, MAKING HISTORY...
Broadmoor
COUNTRY CLUB
MIA ANDO
FIRST CHAIRWOMAN
COMMUNITY DEVELOPMENT
2002
I'D REMEMBER BEING THE BELLE OF THE HANOVER COUNTY FAIR...
I'D REMEMBER THE VIETNAM WAR PROTESTS, AND HOW ALIVE WE ALL FELT, LIKE WE COULD REMAKE THE WORLD...
EACH ONE OF THEM, PERFECT.
A PERFECT MEMORY, IN A SINGLE THING.
HOLDING IT TIGHT TO ME.
LOVING IT, LOVING WHO I USED TO BE...
BEFORE YOU.
HNH.
THEY'RE MORE MY CHILDREN...

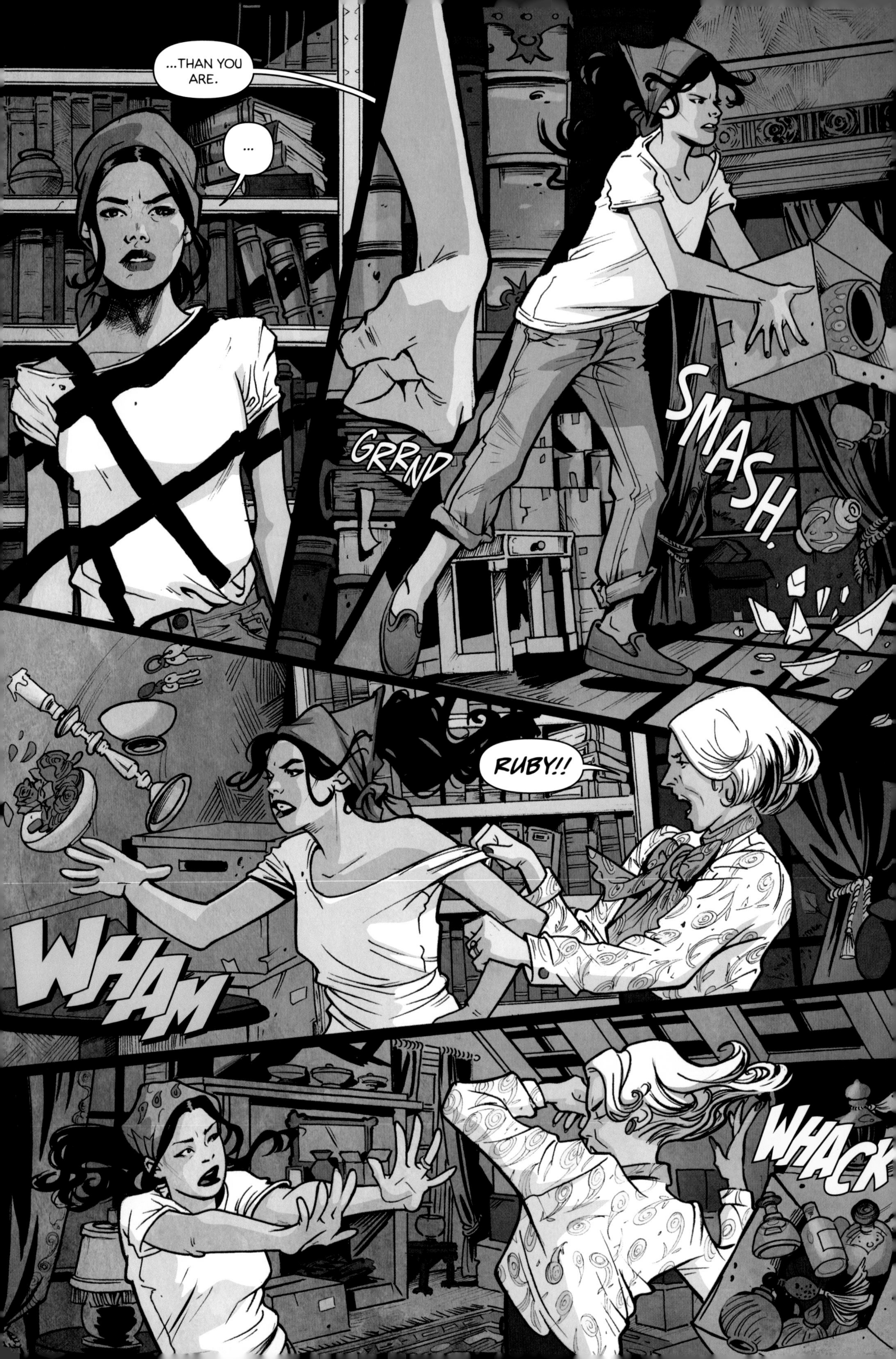
...THAN YOU ARE.
...
GRRND
SMASH.
RUBY!!
WHAM
WHACK

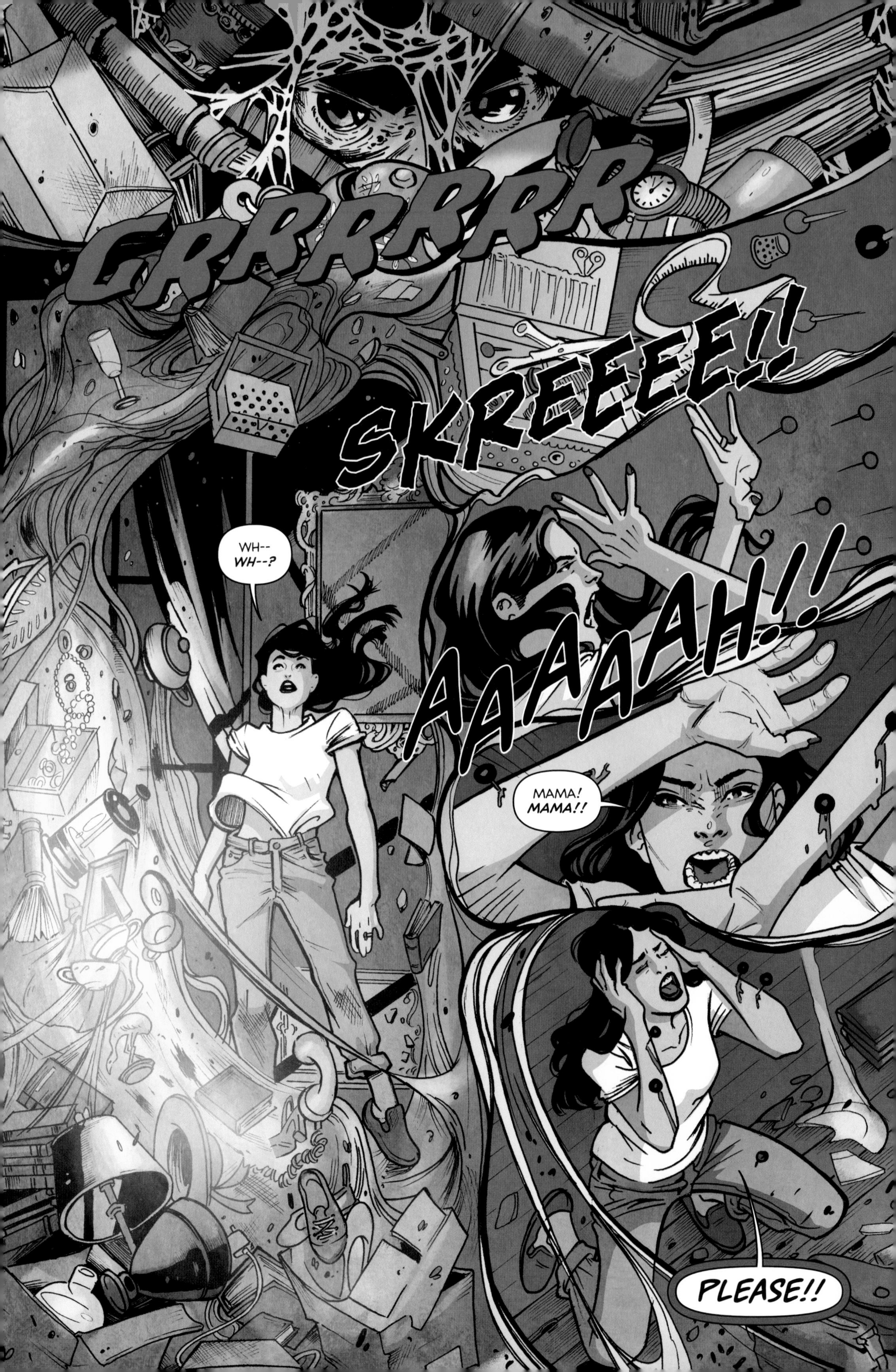
GRRRRRRR
SKREEEEE!!
WH--
WH--?
AAAAAH!!
MAMA!
MAMA!!
PLEASE!!

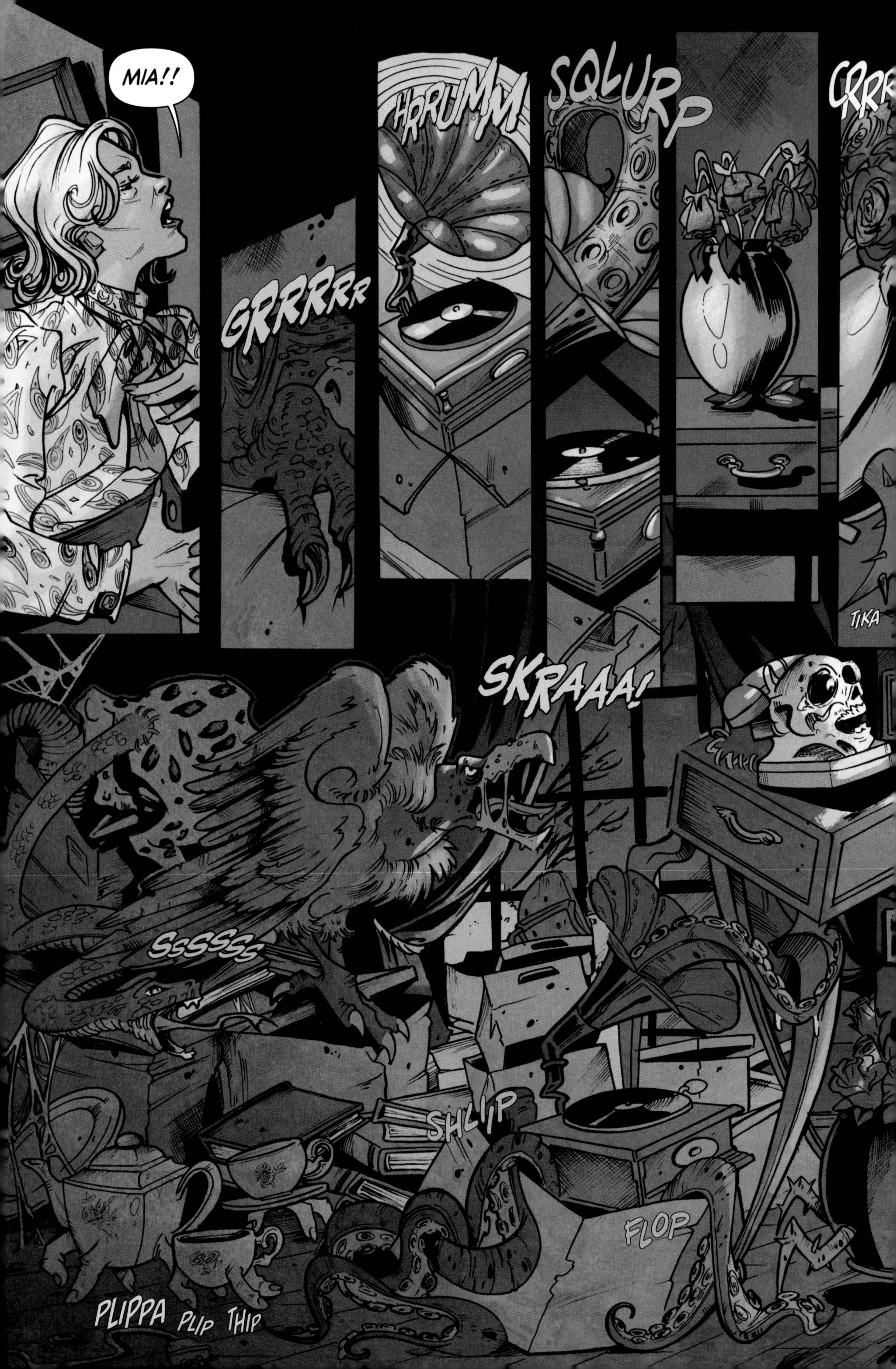
MIA!!
GRRRRrr
HRRUMM
SQLURP
CRRR
TIKA
SKRAAA!
SSSSSS
SHLIP
FLOP
PLIPPA PLIP THIP

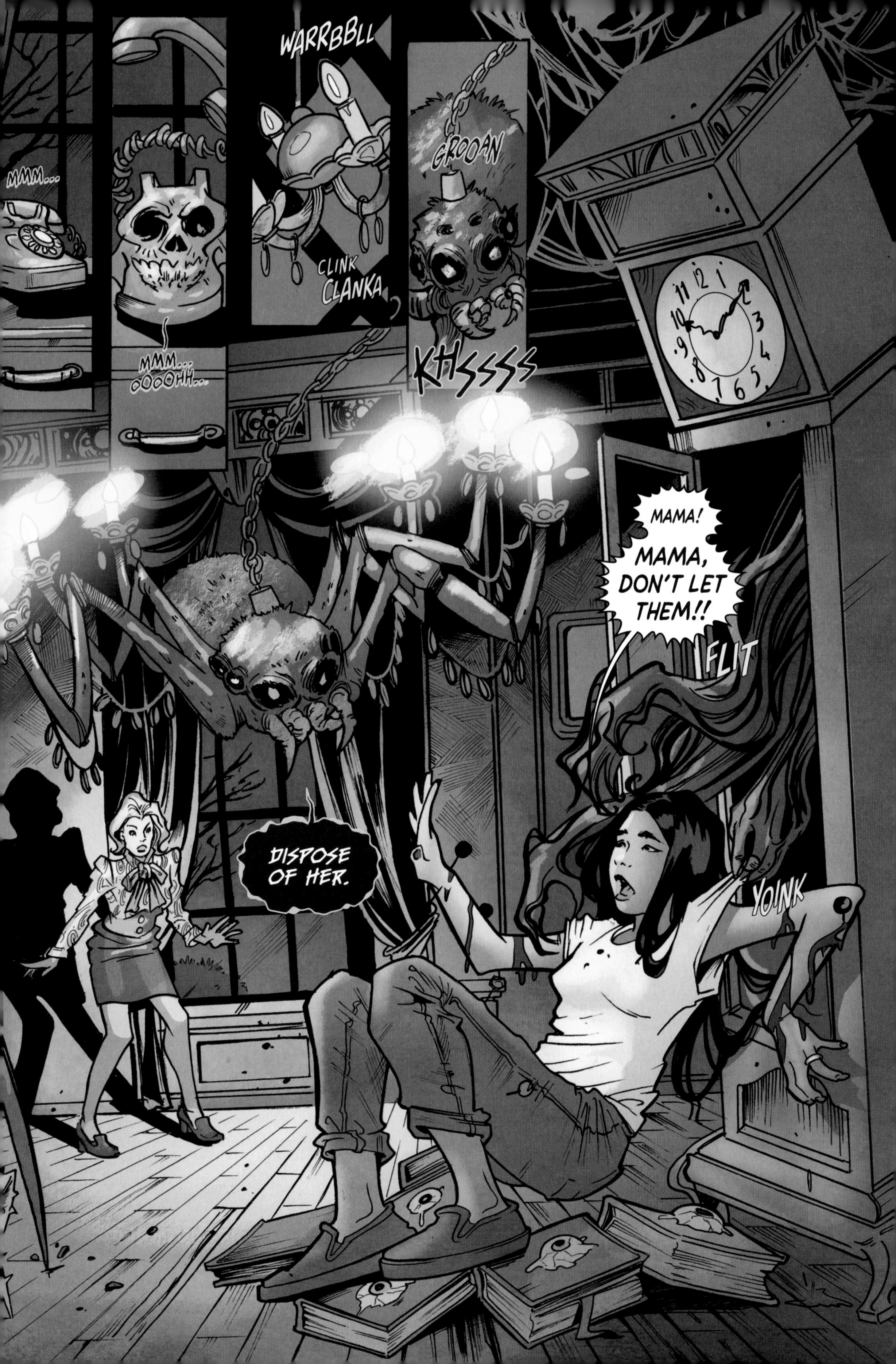
WARRBBLL
MMM...
CLINK
CLANKA
GROOAN
MMM... OOOOHH...
KHSSSS
MAMA!
MAMA, DON'T LET THEM!!
FLIT
DISPOSE OF HER.
YOINK

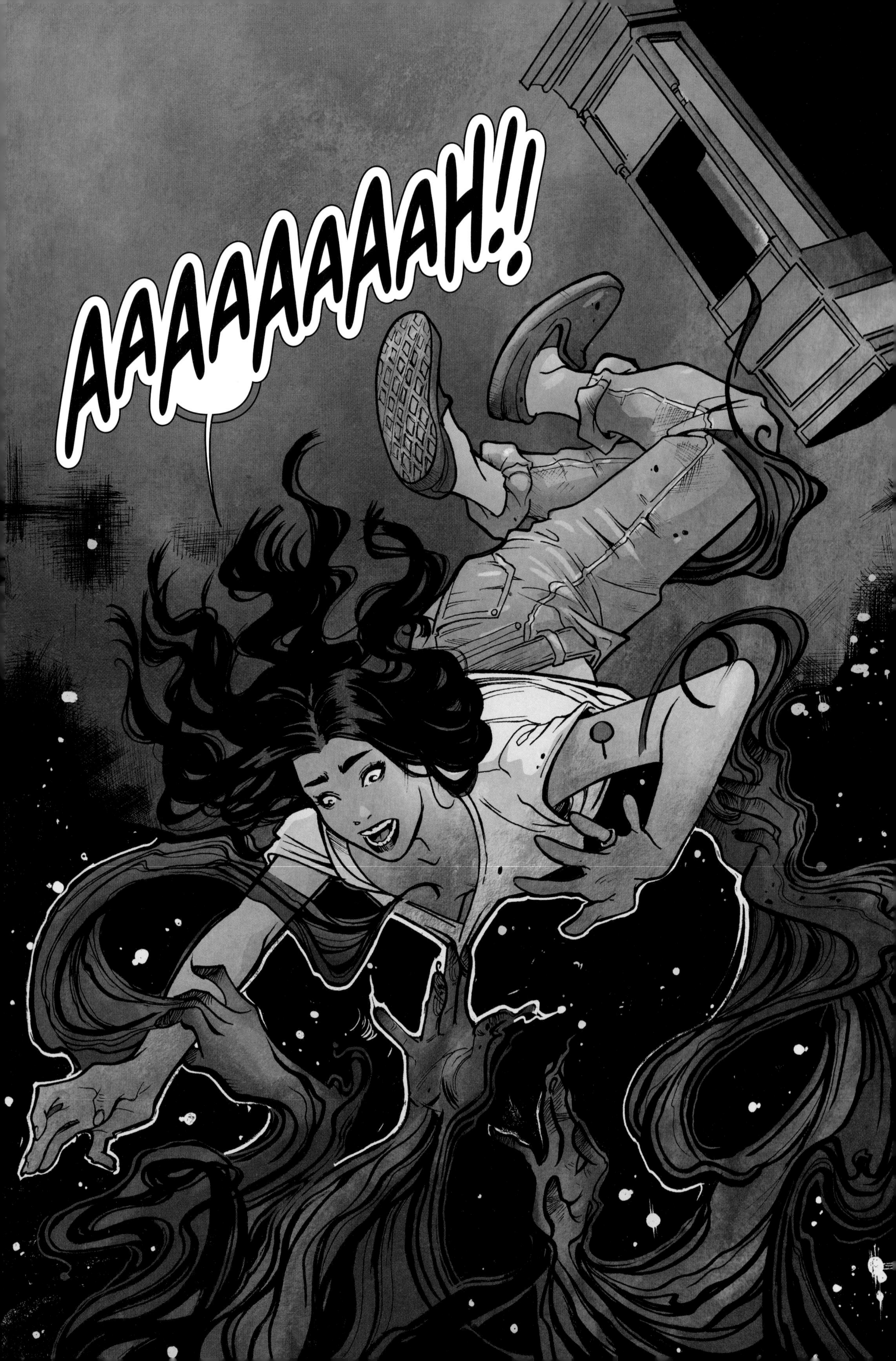
AAAAAAAAH!!

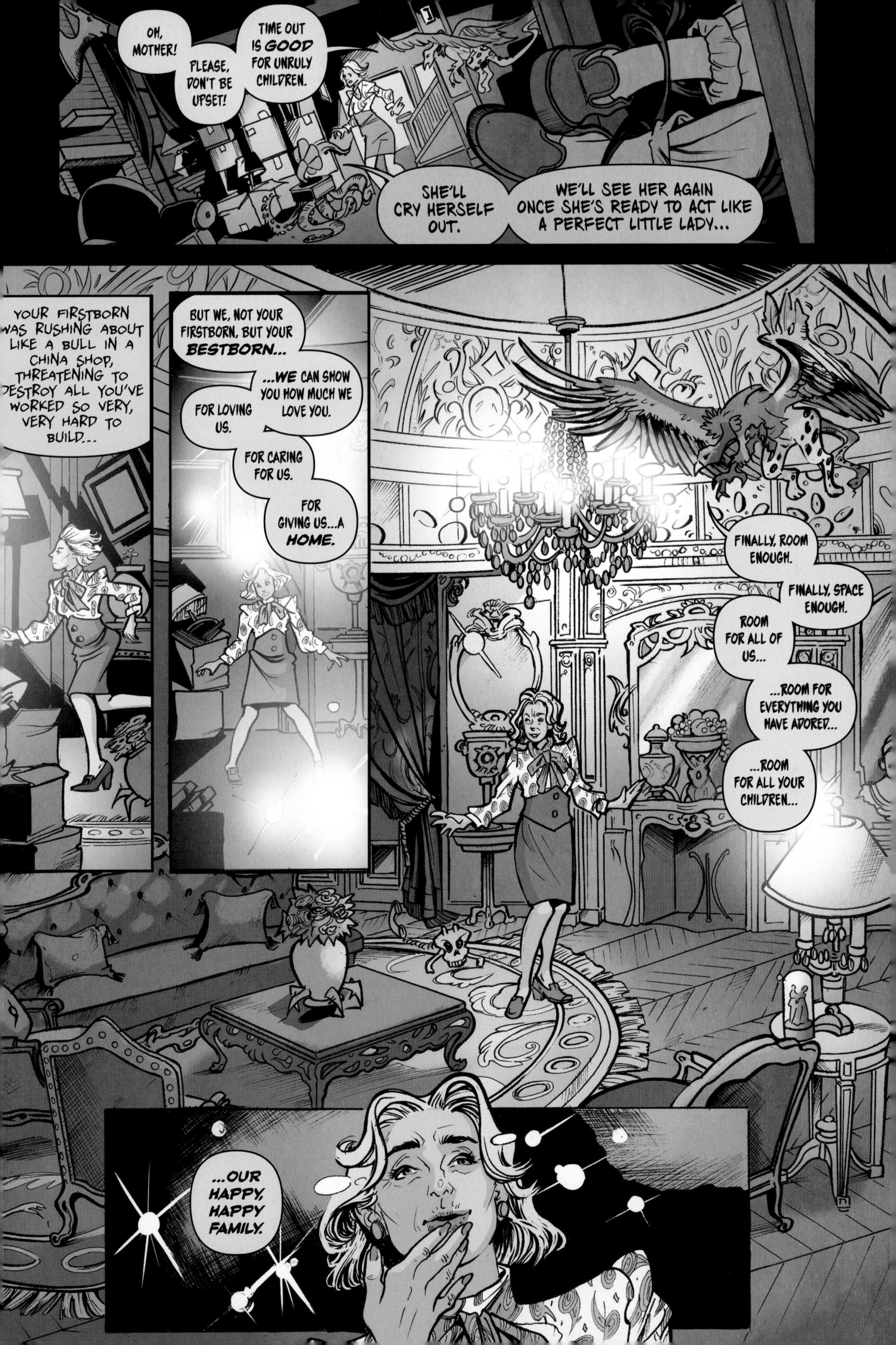
OH, MOTHER!
PLEASE, DON'T BE UPSET!
TIME OUT IS *GOOD* FOR UNRULY CHILDREN.
SHE'LL CRY HERSELF OUT.
WE'LL SEE HER AGAIN ONCE SHE'S READY TO ACT LIKE A PERFECT LITTLE LADY...
YOUR FIRSTBORN WAS RUSHING ABOUT LIKE A BULL IN A CHINA SHOP, THREATENING TO DESTROY ALL YOU'VE WORKED SO VERY, VERY HARD TO BUILD...
BUT WE, NOT YOUR FIRSTBORN, BUT YOUR *BESTBORN*...
...*WE* CAN SHOW YOU HOW MUCH WE LOVE YOU.
FOR LOVING US.
FOR CARING FOR US.
FOR GIVING US...A *HOME*.
FINALLY, ROOM ENOUGH.
FINALLY, SPACE ENOUGH.
ROOM FOR ALL OF US...
...ROOM FOR EVERYTHING YOU HAVE ADORED...
...ROOM FOR ALL YOUR CHILDREN...
...OUR HAPPY, HAPPY FAMILY.

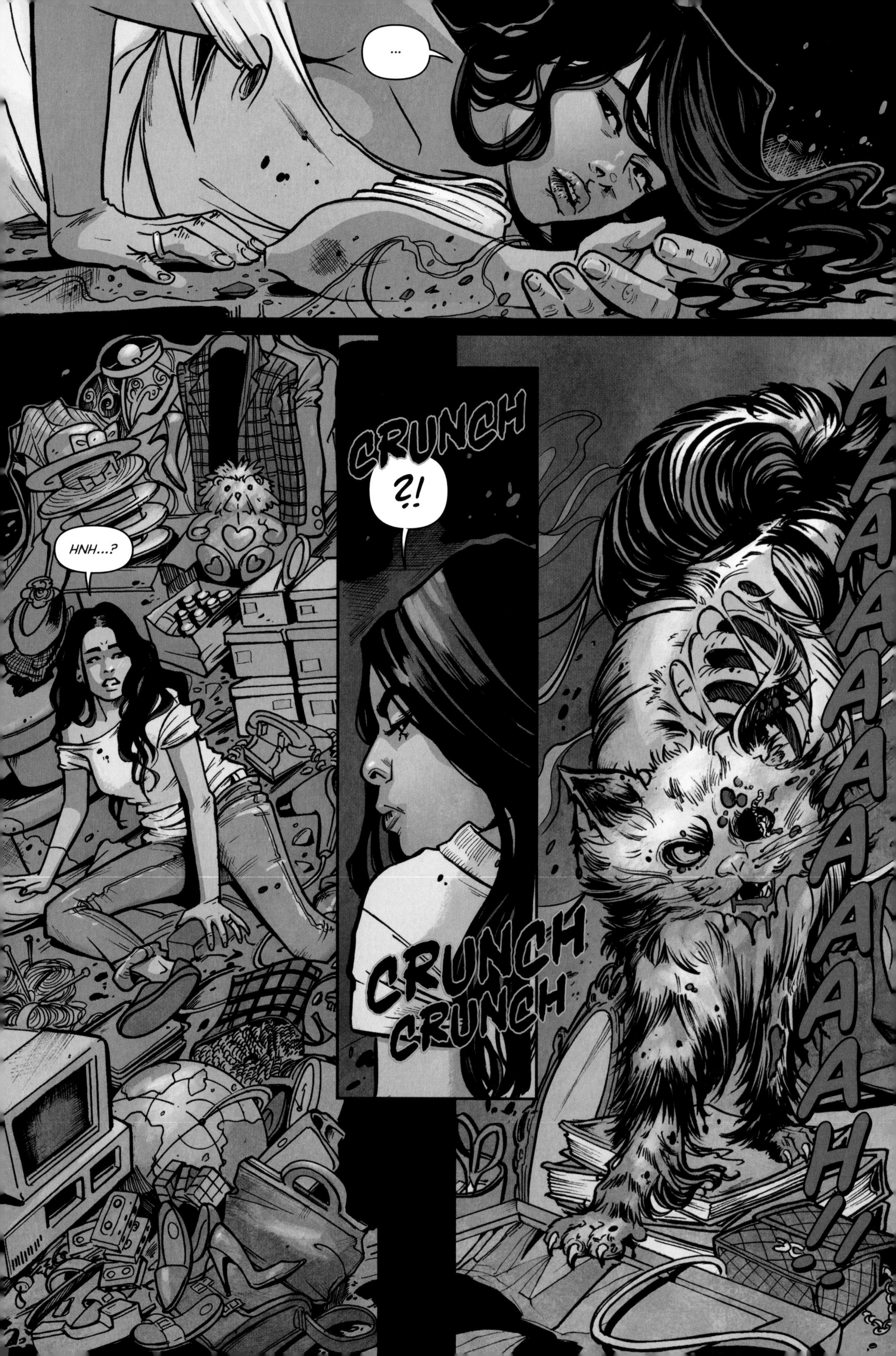
...
HNH...?
CRUNCH
?!
CRUNCH
CRUNCH
AAAAAAAAAAAAAAH!!

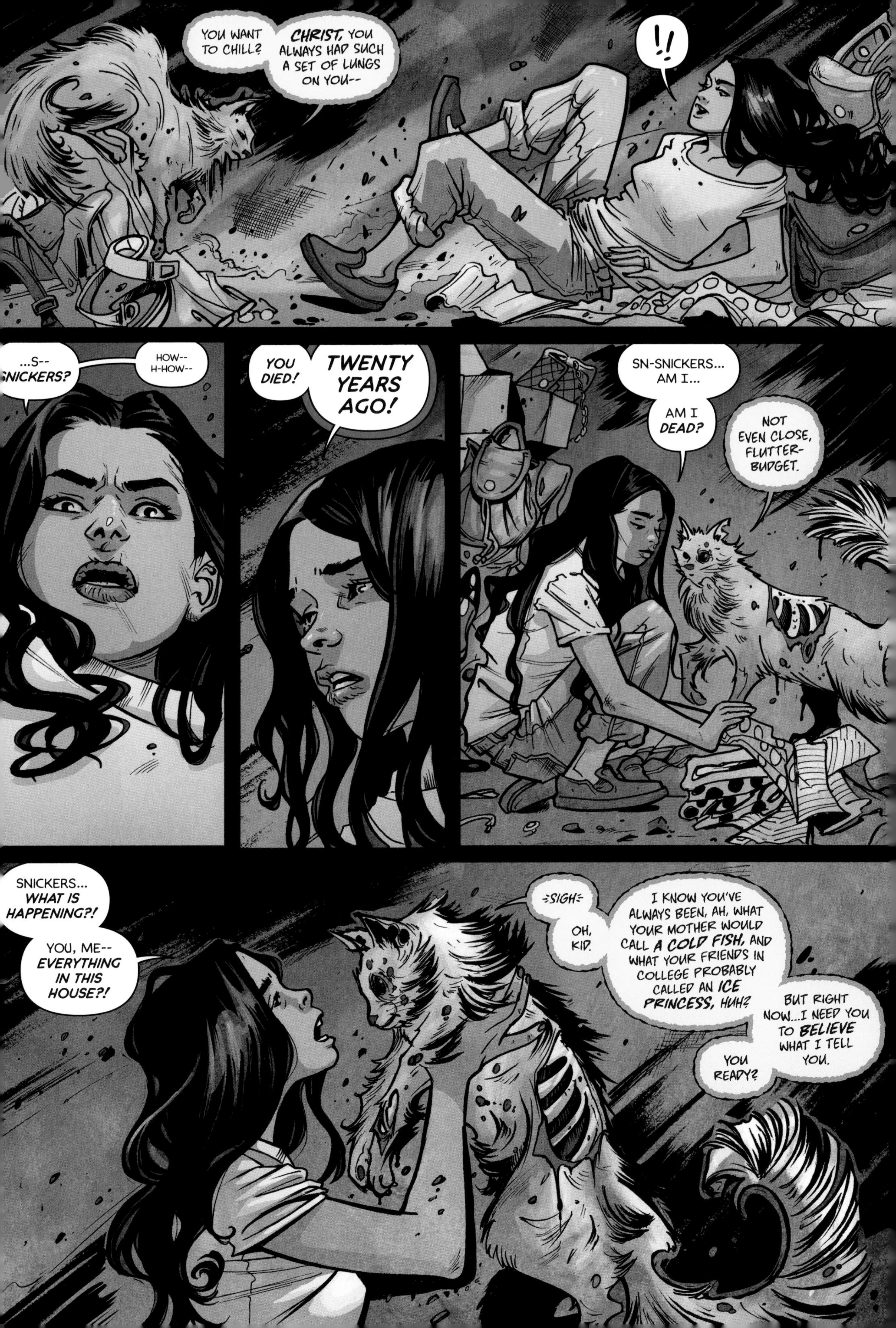
YOU WANT TO CHILL?
CHRIST, YOU ALWAYS HAD SUCH A SET OF LUNGS ON YOU--
!!
...S-- SNICKERS?
HOW-- H-HOW--
YOU DIED!
TWENTY YEARS AGO!
SN-SNICKERS... AM I...
AM I DEAD?
NOT EVEN CLOSE, FLUTTER-BUDGET.
SNICKERS... WHAT IS HAPPENING?!
YOU, ME-- EVERYTHING IN THIS HOUSE?!
SIGH
OH, KID.
I KNOW YOU'VE ALWAYS BEEN, AH, WHAT YOUR MOTHER WOULD CALL A COLD FISH, AND WHAT YOUR FRIENDS IN COLLEGE PROBABLY CALLED AN ICE PRINCESS, HUH?
BUT RIGHT NOW...I NEED YOU TO BELIEVE WHAT I TELL YOU.
YOU READY?

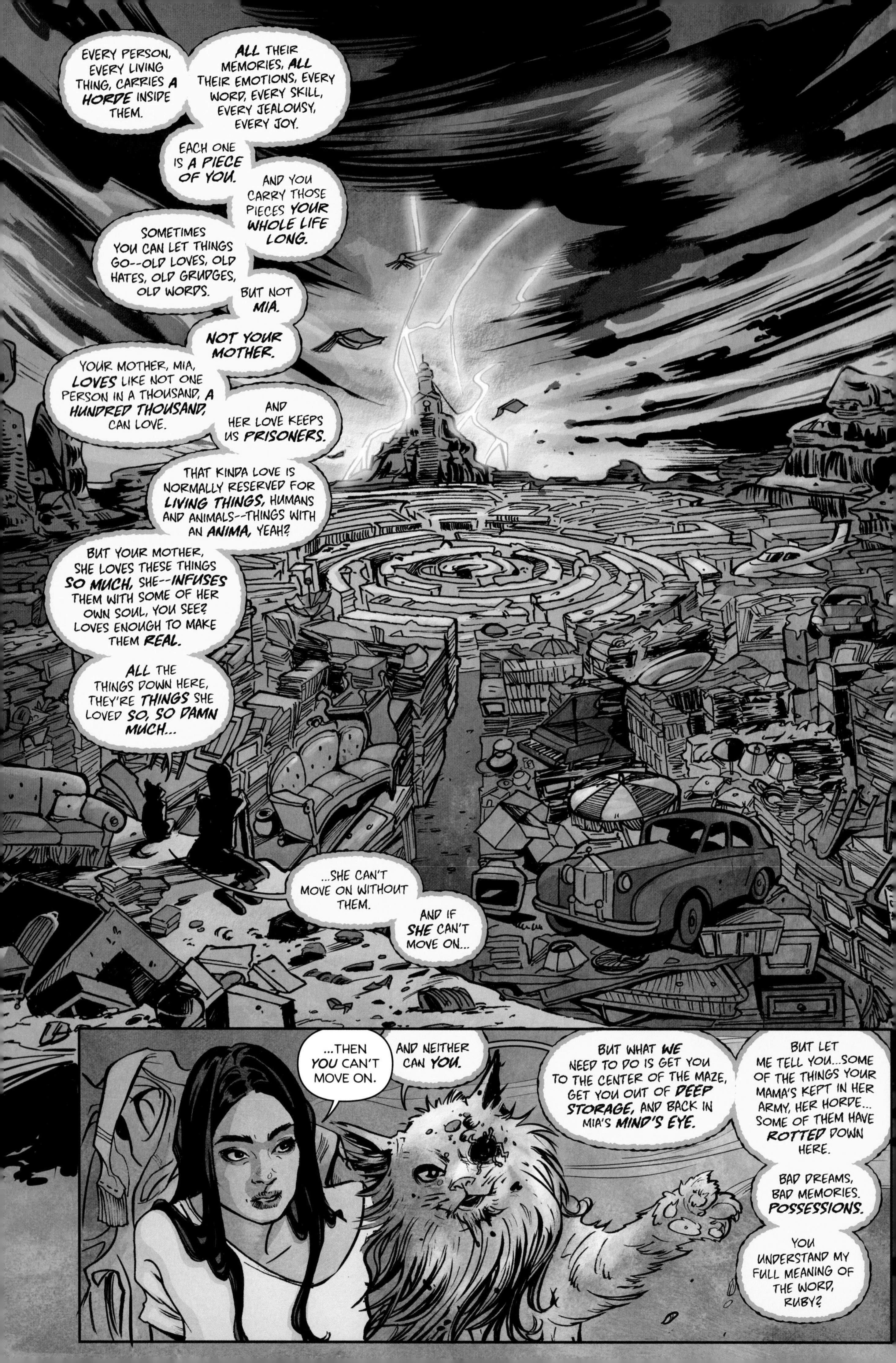
EVERY PERSON, EVERY LIVING THING, CARRIES A HORDE INSIDE THEM.
ALL THEIR MEMORIES, ALL THEIR EMOTIONS, EVERY WORD, EVERY SKILL, EVERY JEALOUSY, EVERY JOY.
EACH ONE IS A PIECE OF YOU.
AND YOU CARRY THOSE PIECES YOUR WHOLE LIFE LONG.
SOMETIMES YOU CAN LET THINGS GO--OLD LOVES, OLD HATES, OLD GRUDGES, OLD WORDS.
BUT NOT MIA.
NOT YOUR MOTHER.
YOUR MOTHER, MIA, LOVES LIKE NOT ONE PERSON IN A THOUSAND, A HUNDRED THOUSAND, CAN LOVE.
AND HER LOVE KEEPS US PRISONERS.
THAT KINDA LOVE IS NORMALLY RESERVED FOR LIVING THINGS, HUMANS AND ANIMALS--THINGS WITH AN ANIMA, YEAH?
BUT YOUR MOTHER, SHE LOVES THESE THINGS SO MUCH, SHE--INFUSES THEM WITH SOME OF HER OWN SOUL, YOU SEE? LOVES ENOUGH TO MAKE THEM REAL.
ALL THE THINGS DOWN HERE, THEY'RE THINGS SHE LOVED SO, SO DAMN MUCH...
...SHE CAN'T MOVE ON WITHOUT THEM.
AND IF SHE CAN'T MOVE ON...
...THEN YOU CAN'T MOVE ON.
AND NEITHER CAN YOU.
BUT WHAT WE NEED TO DO IS GET YOU TO THE CENTER OF THE MAZE, GET YOU OUT OF DEEP STORAGE, AND BACK IN MIA'S MIND'S EYE.
BUT LET ME TELL YOU...SOME OF THE THINGS YOUR MAMA'S KEPT IN HER ARMY, HER HORDE... SOME OF THEM HAVE ROTTED DOWN HERE.
BAD DREAMS, BAD MEMORIES. POSSESSIONS.
YOU UNDERSTAND MY FULL MEANING OF THE WORD, RUBY?

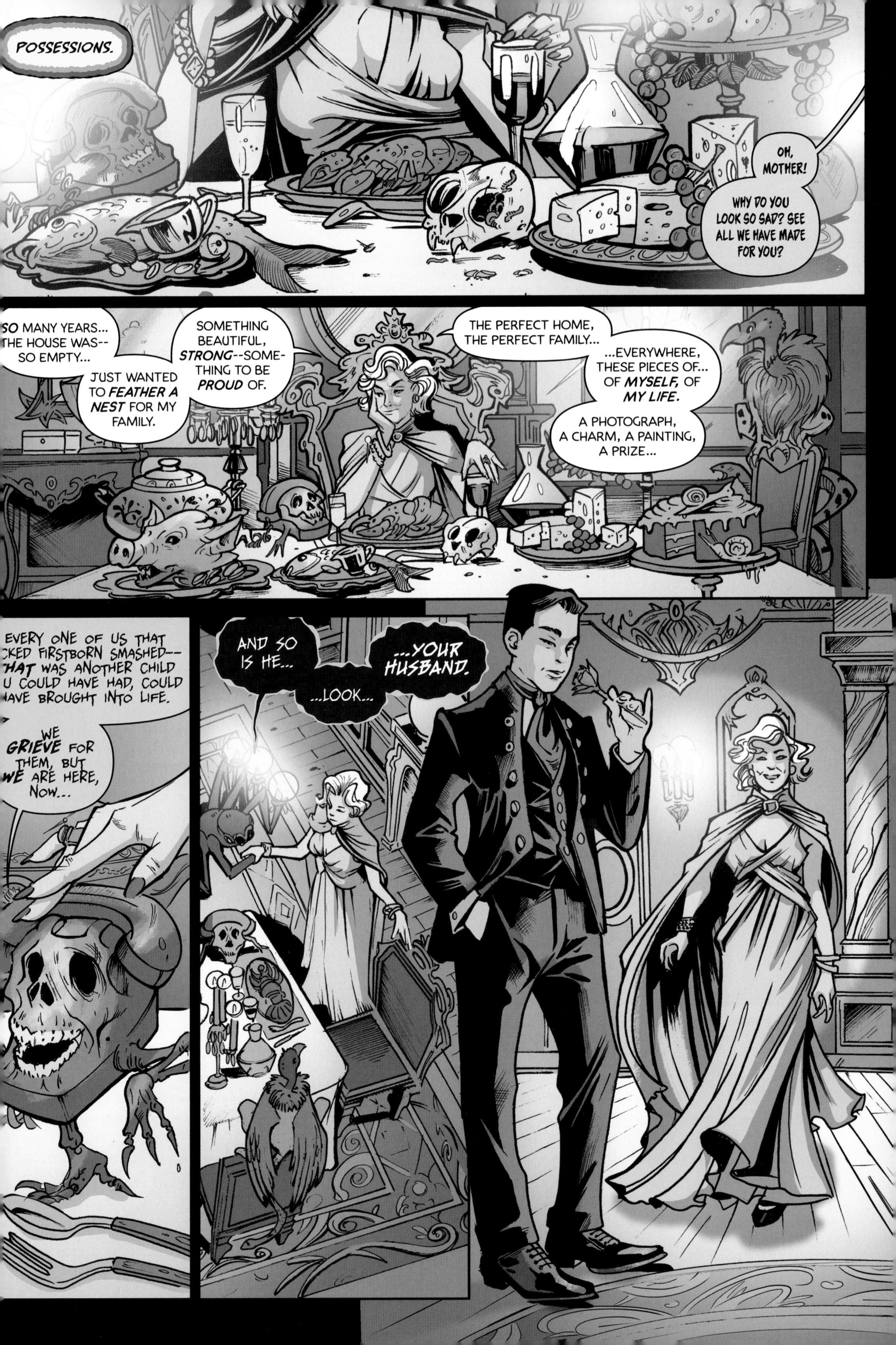
POSSESSIONS.
OH, MOTHER!
WHY DO YOU LOOK SO SAD? SEE ALL WE HAVE MADE FOR YOU?
SO MANY YEARS... THE HOUSE WAS-- SO EMPTY...
JUST WANTED TO FEATHER A NEST FOR MY FAMILY.
SOMETHING BEAUTIFUL, STRONG--SOMETHING TO BE PROUD OF.
THE PERFECT HOME, THE PERFECT FAMILY...
...EVERYWHERE, THESE PIECES OF... OF MYSELF, OF MY LIFE.
A PHOTOGRAPH, A CHARM, A PAINTING, A PRIZE...
EVERY ONE OF US THAT CKED FIRSTBORN SMASHED-- THAT WAS ANOTHER CHILD U COULD HAVE HAD, COULD AVE BROUGHT INTO LIFE.
WE GRIEVE FOR THEM, BUT WE ARE HERE, NOW...
AND SO IS HE...
...LOOK...
...YOUR HUSBAND.

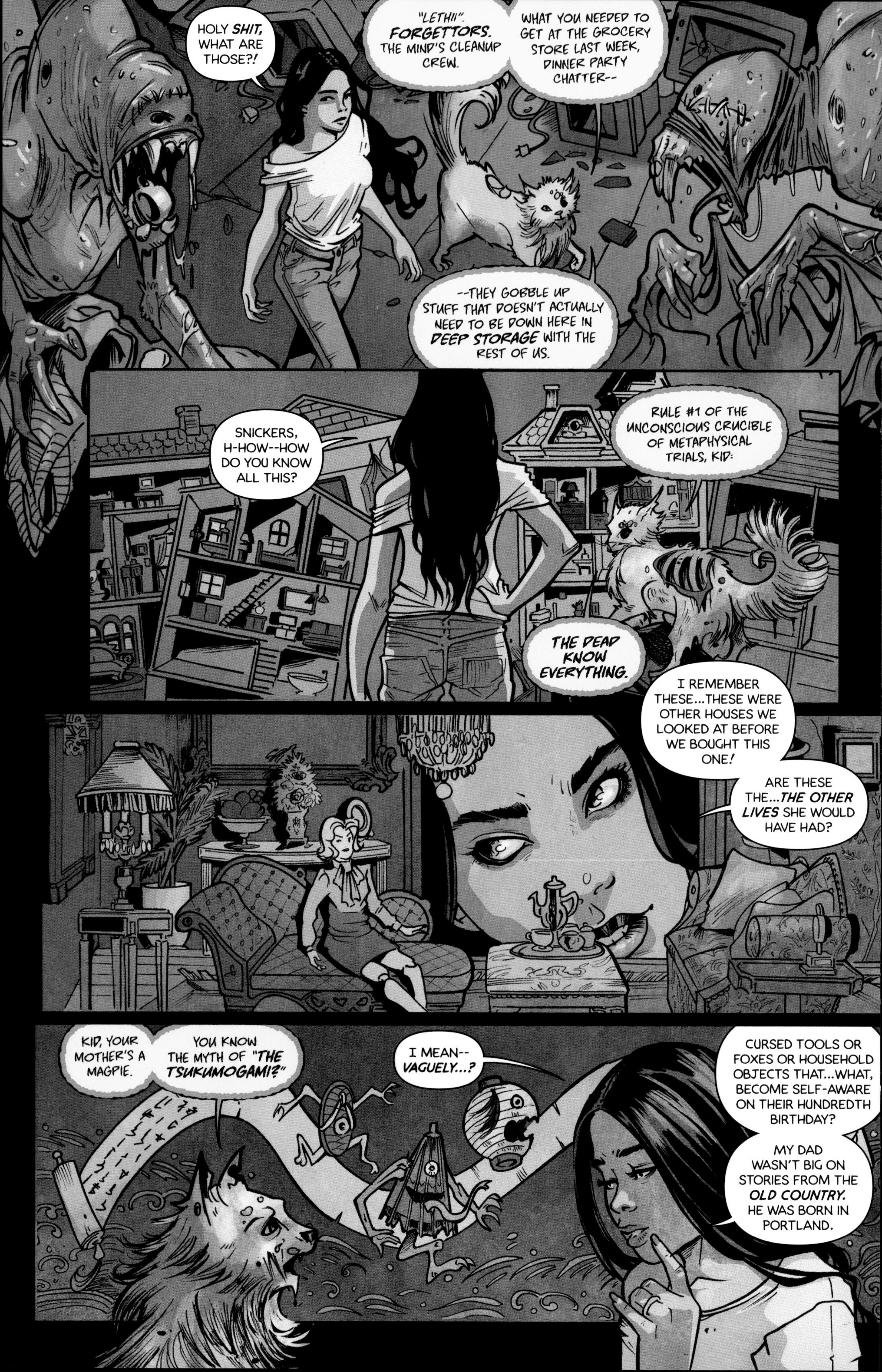
HOLY SHIT, WHAT ARE THOSE?!
"LETHII". FORGETTORS. THE MIND'S CLEANUP CREW.
WHAT YOU NEEDED TO GET AT THE GROCERY STORE LAST WEEK, DINNER PARTY CHATTER--
--THEY GOBBLE UP STUFF THAT DOESN'T ACTUALLY NEED TO BE DOWN HERE IN DEEP STORAGE WITH THE REST OF US.
SNICKERS, H-HOW--HOW DO YOU KNOW ALL THIS?
RULE #1 OF THE UNCONSCIOUS CRUCIBLE OF METAPHYSICAL TRIALS, KID:
THE DEAD KNOW EVERYTHING.
I REMEMBER THESE...THESE WERE OTHER HOUSES WE LOOKED AT BEFORE WE BOUGHT THIS ONE!
ARE THESE THE...THE OTHER LIVES SHE WOULD HAVE HAD?
KID, YOUR MOTHER'S A MAGPIE.
YOU KNOW THE MYTH OF "THE TSUKUMOGAMI?"
I MEAN--VAGUELY...?
CURSED TOOLS OR FOXES OR HOUSEHOLD OBJECTS THAT...WHAT, BECOME SELF-AWARE ON THEIR HUNDREDTH BIRTHDAY?
MY DAD WASN'T BIG ON STORIES FROM THE OLD COUNTRY. HE WAS BORN IN PORTLAND.

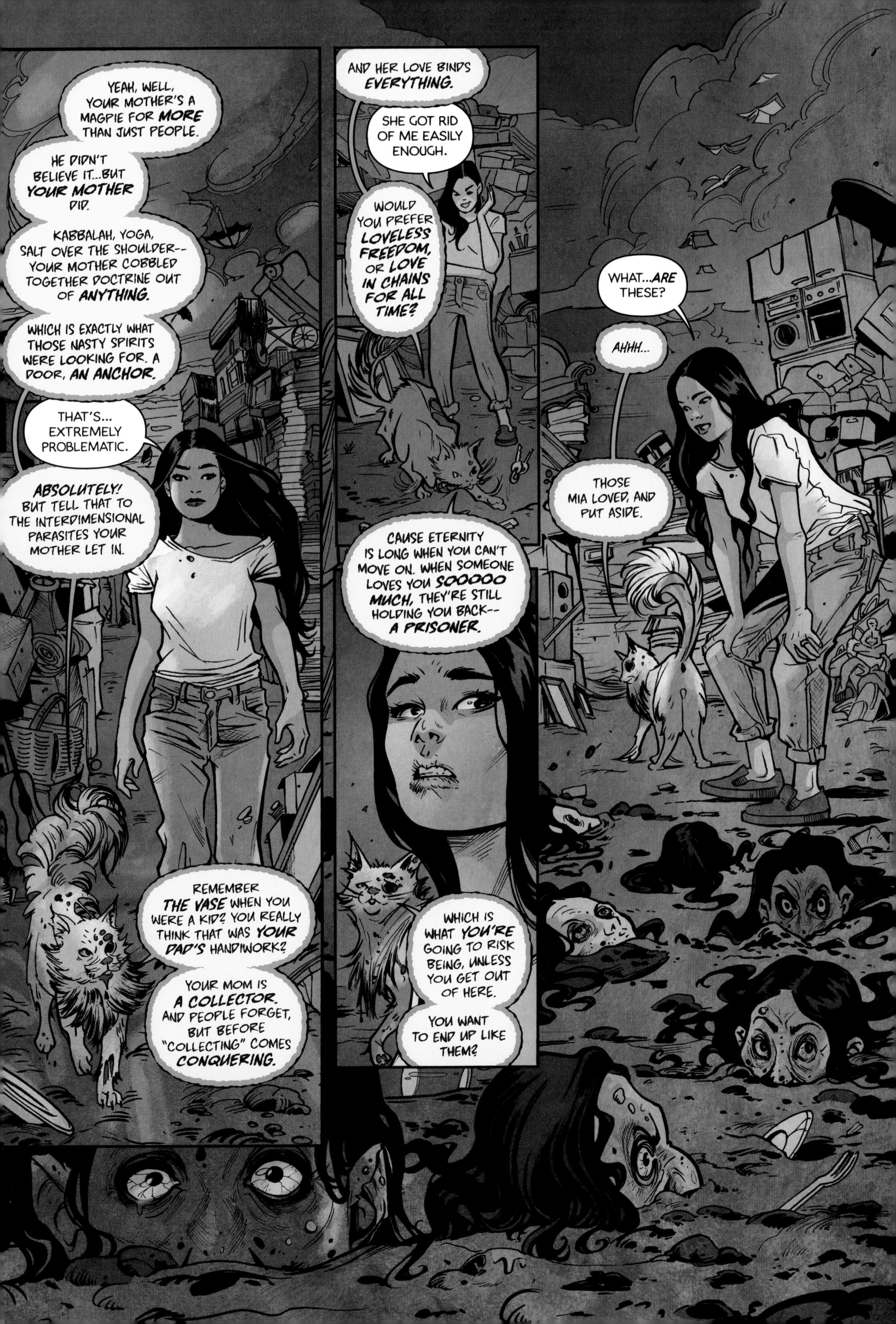

YEAH, WELL, YOUR MOTHER'S A MAGPIE FOR MORE THAN JUST PEOPLE.
HE DIDN'T BELIEVE IT...BUT YOUR MOTHER DID.
KABBALAH, YOGA, SALT OVER THE SHOULDER-- YOUR MOTHER COBBLED TOGETHER DOCTRINE OUT OF ANYTHING.
WHICH IS EXACTLY WHAT THOSE NASTY SPIRITS WERE LOOKING FOR. A DOOR, AN ANCHOR.
THAT'S... EXTREMELY PROBLEMATIC.
ABSOLUTELY! BUT TELL THAT TO THE INTERDIMENSIONAL PARASITES YOUR MOTHER LET IN.
REMEMBER THE VASE WHEN YOU WERE A KID? YOU REALLY THINK THAT WAS YOUR DAD'S HANDIWORK?
YOUR MOM IS A COLLECTOR. AND PEOPLE FORGET, BUT BEFORE "COLLECTING" COMES CONQUERING.
AND HER LOVE BINDS EVERYTHING.
SHE GOT RID OF ME EASILY ENOUGH.
WOULD YOU PREFER LOVELESS FREEDOM, OR LOVE IN CHAINS FOR ALL TIME?
CAUSE ETERNITY IS LONG WHEN YOU CAN'T MOVE ON. WHEN SOMEONE LOVES YOU SOOOOO MUCH, THEY'RE STILL HOLDING YOU BACK-- A PRISONER.
WHICH IS WHAT YOU'RE GOING TO RISK BEING, UNLESS YOU GET OUT OF HERE.
YOU WANT TO END UP LIKE THEM?
WHAT...ARE THESE?
AHHH...
THOSE MIA LOVED, AND PUT ASIDE.

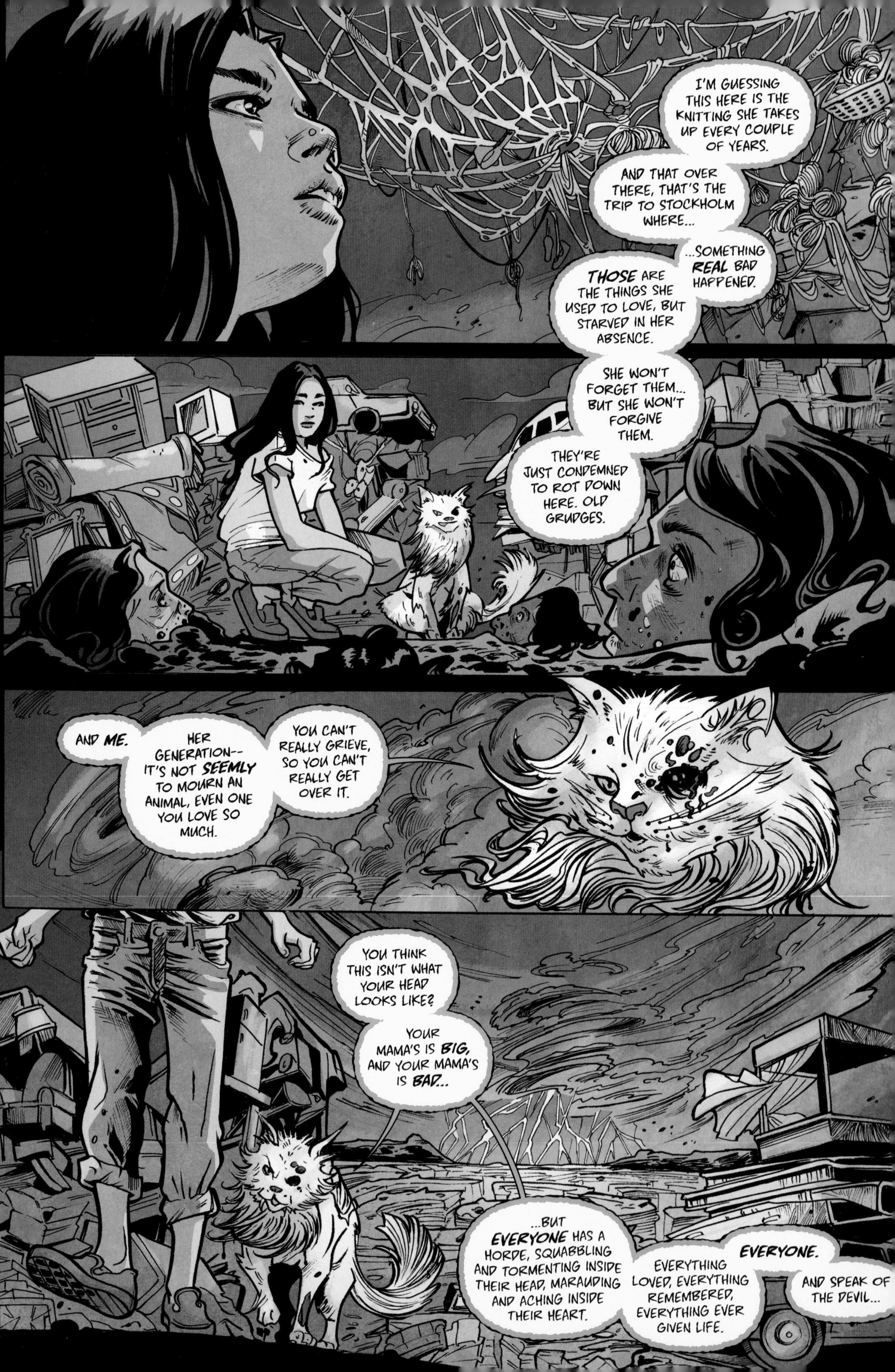
I'M GUESSING THIS HERE IS THE KNITTING SHE TAKES UP EVERY COUPLE OF YEARS.
AND THAT OVER THERE, THAT'S THE TRIP TO STOCKHOLM WHERE...
...SOMETHING **REAL** BAD HAPPENED.
THOSE ARE THE THINGS SHE USED TO LOVE, BUT STARVED IN HER ABSENCE.
SHE WON'T FORGET THEM... BUT SHE WON'T FORGIVE THEM.
THEY'RE JUST CONDEMNED TO ROT DOWN HERE. OLD GRUDGES.
AND **ME.**
HER GENERATION-- IT'S NOT **SEEMLY** TO MOURN AN ANIMAL, EVEN ONE YOU LOVE SO MUCH.
YOU CAN'T REALLY GRIEVE, SO YOU CAN'T REALLY GET OVER IT.
YOU THINK THIS ISN'T WHAT YOUR HEAD LOOKS LIKE?
YOUR MAMA'S IS **BIG,** AND YOUR MAMA'S IS **BAD...**
...BUT **EVERYONE** HAS A HORDE, SQUABBLING AND TORMENTING INSIDE THEIR HEAD, MARAUDING AND ACHING INSIDE THEIR HEART.
EVERYONE.
EVERYTHING LOVED, EVERYTHING REMEMBERED, EVERYTHING EVER GIVEN LIFE.
AND SPEAK OF THE DEVIL...

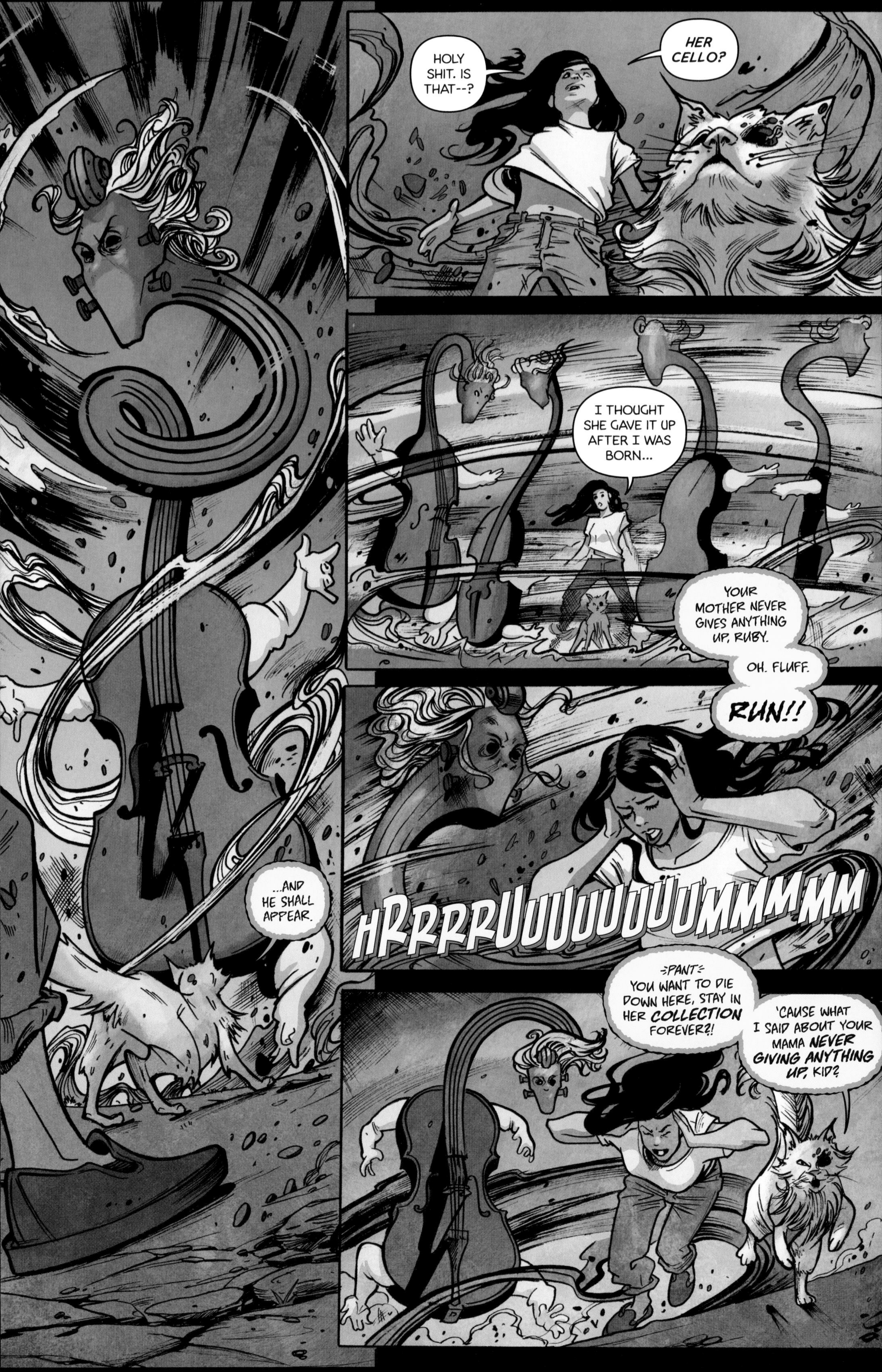

HOLY SHIT. IS THAT--?
HER CELLO?
I THOUGHT SHE GAVE IT UP AFTER I WAS BORN...
YOUR MOTHER NEVER GIVES ANYTHING UP, RUBY.
OH. FLUFF.
RUN!!
...AND HE SHALL APPEAR.
HRRRRUUUUUUUUMMMMM
=PANT=
YOU WANT TO DIE DOWN HERE, STAY IN HER COLLECTION FOREVER?!
'CAUSE WHAT I SAID ABOUT YOUR MAMA NEVER GIVING ANYTHING UP, KID?

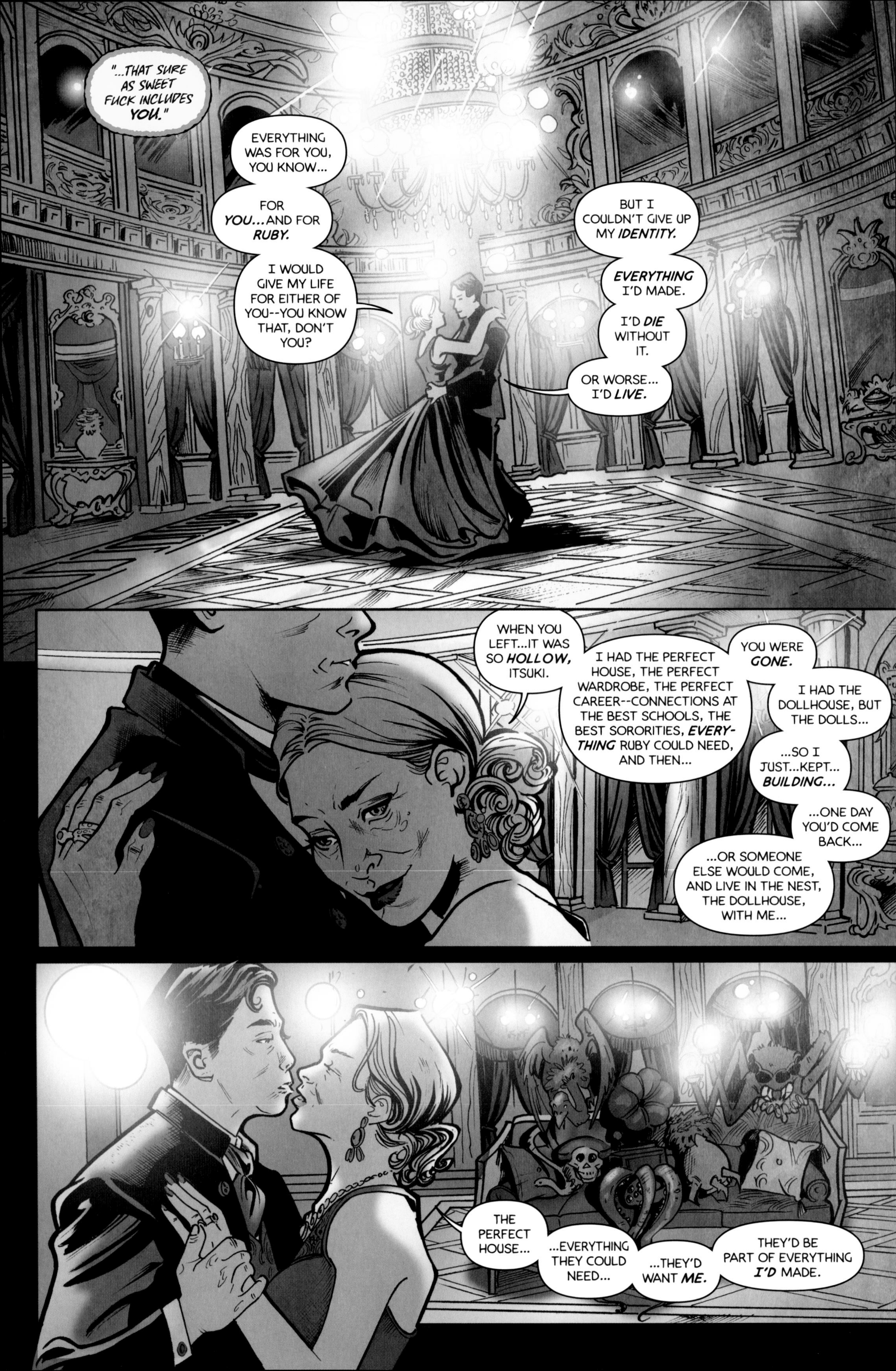
"...THAT SURE AS SWEET FUCK INCLUDES YOU."
EVERYTHING WAS FOR YOU, YOU KNOW...
FOR YOU...AND FOR RUBY.
I WOULD GIVE MY LIFE FOR EITHER OF YOU--YOU KNOW THAT, DON'T YOU?
BUT I COULDN'T GIVE UP MY IDENTITY.
EVERYTHING I'D MADE.
I'D DIE WITHOUT IT.
OR WORSE... I'D LIVE.
WHEN YOU LEFT...IT WAS SO HOLLOW, ITSUKI.
I HAD THE PERFECT HOUSE, THE PERFECT WARDROBE, THE PERFECT CAREER--CONNECTIONS AT THE BEST SCHOOLS, THE BEST SORORITIES, EVERY-THING RUBY COULD NEED, AND THEN...
YOU WERE GONE.
I HAD THE DOLLHOUSE, BUT THE DOLLS...
...SO I JUST...KEPT... BUILDING...
...ONE DAY YOU'D COME BACK...
...OR SOMEONE ELSE WOULD COME, AND LIVE IN THE NEST, THE DOLLHOUSE, WITH ME...
THE PERFECT HOUSE...
...EVERYTHING THEY COULD NEED...
...THEY'D WANT ME.
THEY'D BE PART OF EVERYTHING I'D MADE.

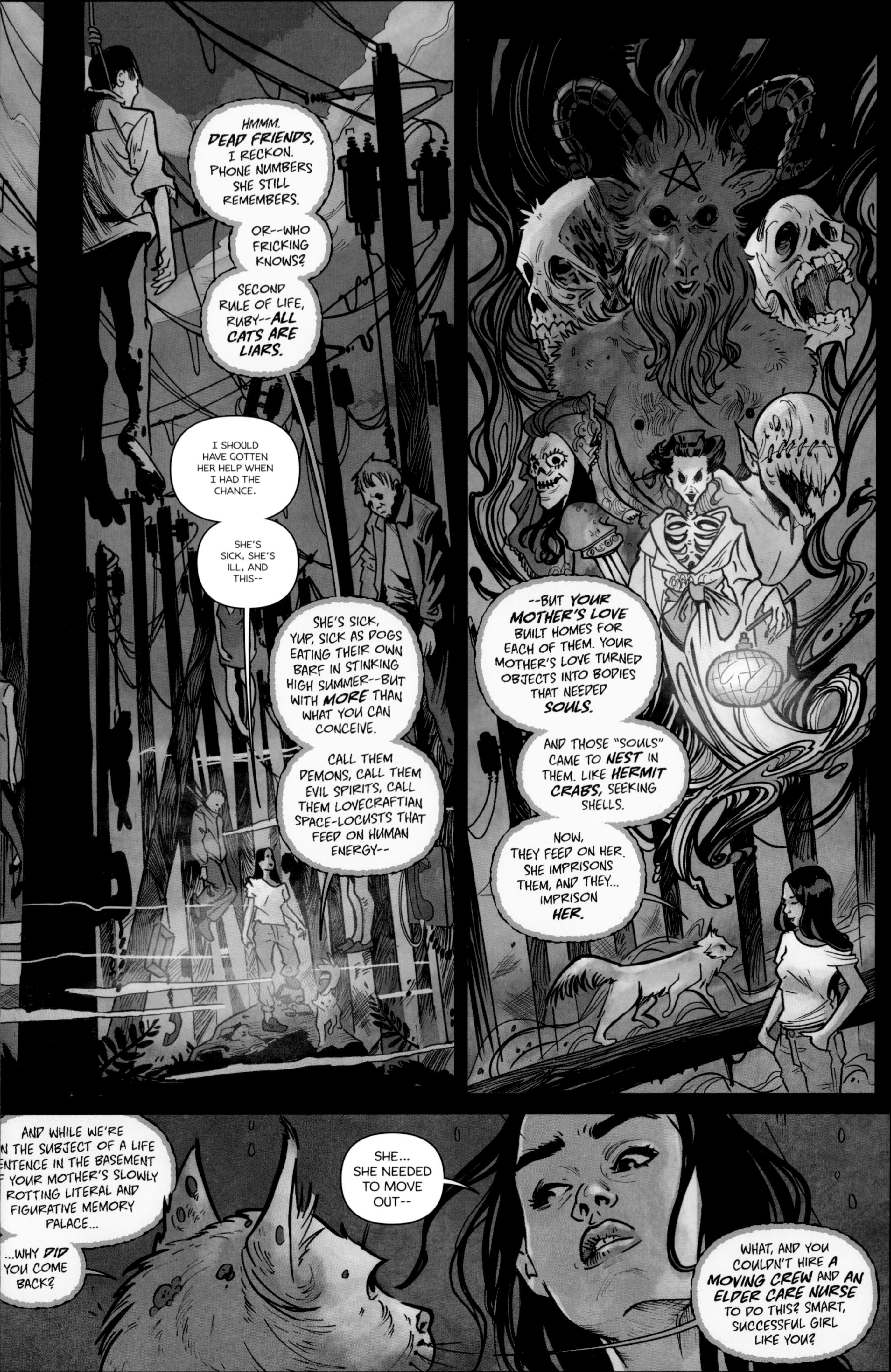

HMMM. DEAD FRIENDS, I RECKON. PHONE NUMBERS SHE STILL REMEMBERS.
OR--WHO FRICKING KNOWS?
SECOND RULE OF LIFE, RUBY--ALL CATS ARE LIARS.
I SHOULD HAVE GOTTEN HER HELP WHEN I HAD THE CHANCE.
SHE'S SICK, SHE'S ILL, AND THIS--
SHE'S SICK, YUP, SICK AS DOGS EATING THEIR OWN BARF IN STINKING HIGH SUMMER--BUT WITH MORE THAN WHAT YOU CAN CONCEIVE.
CALL THEM DEMONS, CALL THEM EVIL SPIRITS, CALL THEM LOVECRAFTIAN SPACE-LOCUSTS THAT FEED ON HUMAN ENERGY--
--BUT YOUR MOTHER'S LOVE BUILT HOMES FOR EACH OF THEM. YOUR MOTHER'S LOVE TURNED OBJECTS INTO BODIES THAT NEEDED SOULS.
AND THOSE "SOULS" CAME TO NEST IN THEM. LIKE HERMIT CRABS, SEEKING SHELLS.
NOW, THEY FEED ON HER. SHE IMPRISONS THEM, AND THEY... IMPRISON HER.
AND WHILE WE'RE N THE SUBJECT OF A LIFE ENTENCE IN THE BASEMENT F YOUR MOTHER'S SLOWLY ROTTING LITERAL AND FIGURATIVE MEMORY PALACE...
...WHY DID YOU COME BACK?
SHE... SHE NEEDED TO MOVE OUT--
WHAT, AND YOU COULDN'T HIRE A MOVING CREW AND AN ELDER CARE NURSE TO DO THIS? SMART, SUCCESSFUL GIRL LIKE YOU?

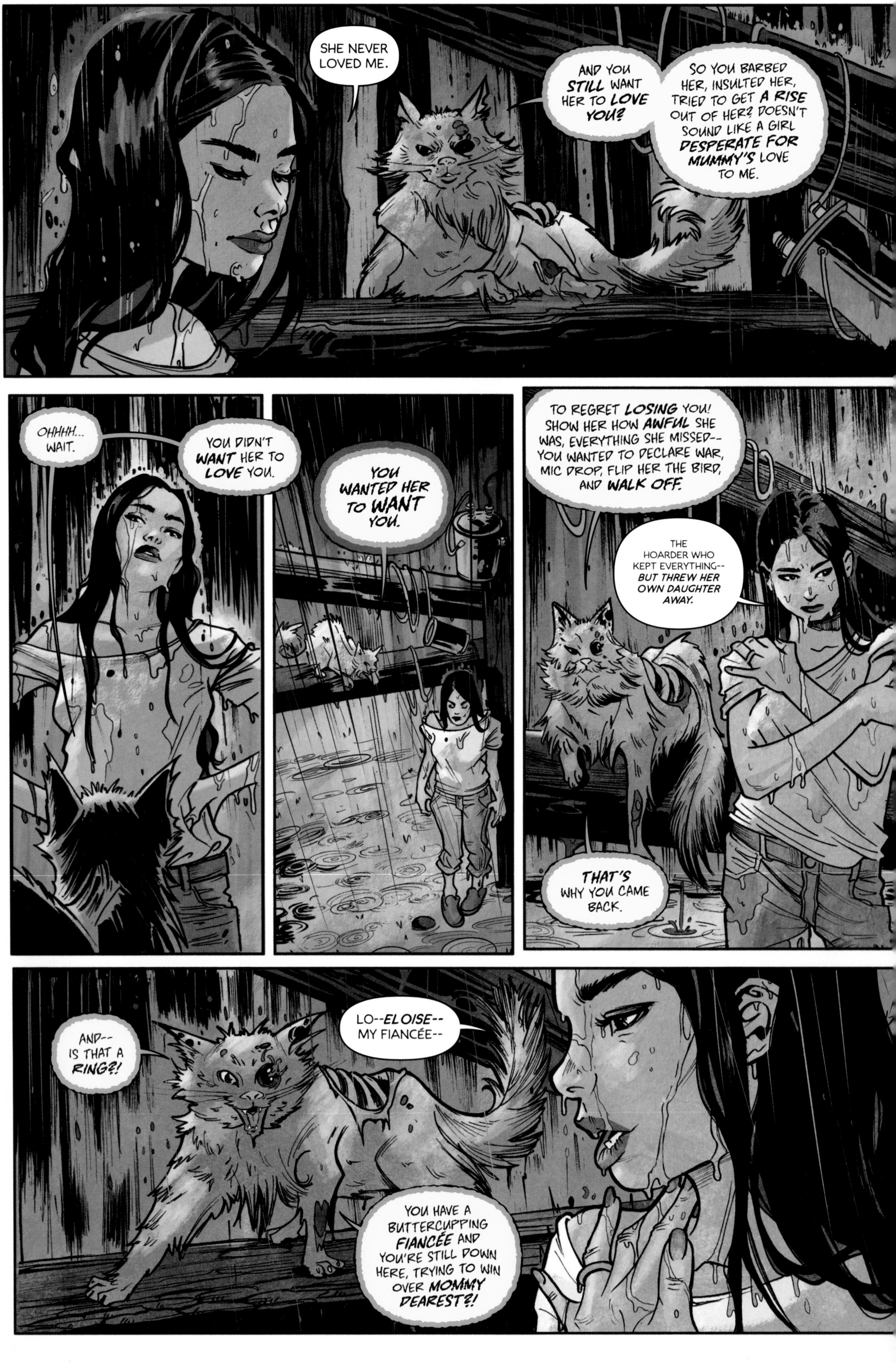

SHE NEVER LOVED ME.
AND YOU STILL WANT HER TO LOVE YOU?
SO YOU BARBED HER, INSULTED HER, TRIED TO GET A RISE OUT OF HER? DOESN'T SOUND LIKE A GIRL DESPERATE FOR MUMMY'S LOVE TO ME.
OHHHH... WAIT.
YOU DIDN'T WANT HER TO LOVE YOU.
YOU WANTED HER TO WANT YOU.
TO REGRET LOSING YOU! SHOW HER HOW AWFUL SHE WAS, EVERYTHING SHE MISSED-- YOU WANTED TO DECLARE WAR, MIC DROP, FLIP HER THE BIRD, AND WALK OFF.
THE HOARDER WHO KEPT EVERYTHING-- BUT THREW HER OWN DAUGHTER AWAY.
THAT'S WHY YOU CAME BACK.
AND-- IS THAT A RING?!
LO--ELOISE-- MY FIANCÉE--
YOU HAVE A BUTTERCUPPING FIANCÉE AND YOU'RE STILL DOWN HERE, TRYING TO WIN OVER MOMMY DEAREST?!

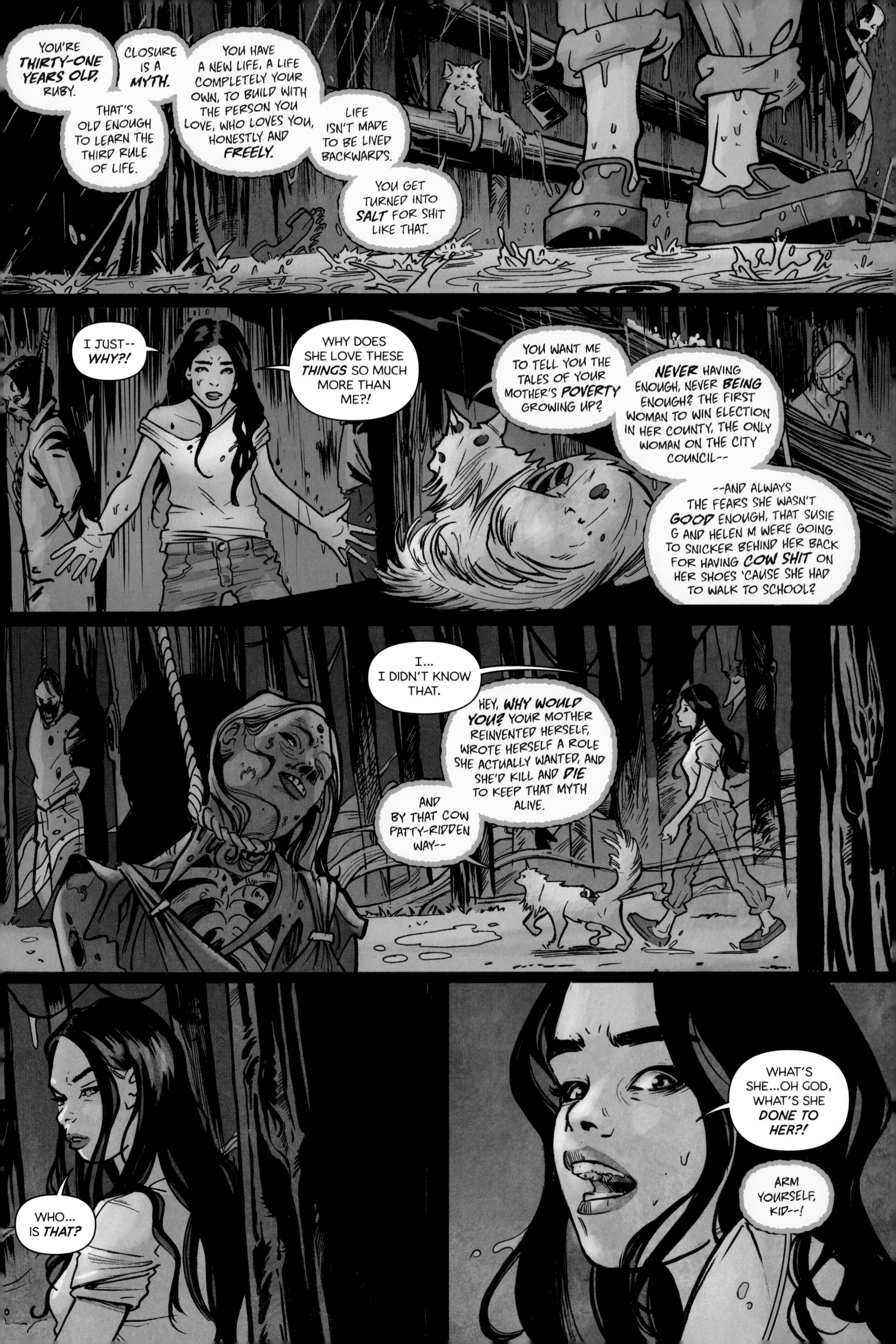
YOU'RE THIRTY-ONE YEARS OLD, RUBY.
THAT'S OLD ENOUGH TO LEARN THE THIRD RULE OF LIFE.
CLOSURE IS A MYTH.
YOU HAVE A NEW LIFE, A LIFE COMPLETELY YOUR OWN, TO BUILD WITH THE PERSON YOU LOVE, WHO LOVES YOU, HONESTLY AND FREELY.
LIFE ISN'T MADE TO BE LIVED BACKWARDS.
YOU GET TURNED INTO SALT FOR SHIT LIKE THAT.
I JUST-- WHY?!
WHY DOES SHE LOVE THESE THINGS SO MUCH MORE THAN ME?!
YOU WANT ME TO TELL YOU THE TALES OF YOUR MOTHER'S POVERTY GROWING UP?
NEVER HAVING ENOUGH, NEVER BEING ENOUGH? THE FIRST WOMAN TO WIN ELECTION IN HER COUNTY, THE ONLY WOMAN ON THE CITY COUNCIL--
--AND ALWAYS THE FEARS SHE WASN'T GOOD ENOUGH, THAT SUSIE G AND HELEN M WERE GOING TO SNICKER BEHIND HER BACK FOR HAVING COW SHIT ON HER SHOES 'CAUSE SHE HAD TO WALK TO SCHOOL?
I... I DIDN'T KNOW THAT.
HEY, WHY WOULD YOU? YOUR MOTHER REINVENTED HERSELF, WROTE HERSELF A ROLE SHE ACTUALLY WANTED, AND SHE'D KILL AND DIE TO KEEP THAT MYTH ALIVE.
AND BY THAT COW PATTY-RIDDEN WAY--
WHO... IS THAT?
WHAT'S SHE...OH GOD, WHAT'S SHE DONE TO HER?!
ARM YOURSELF, KID--!

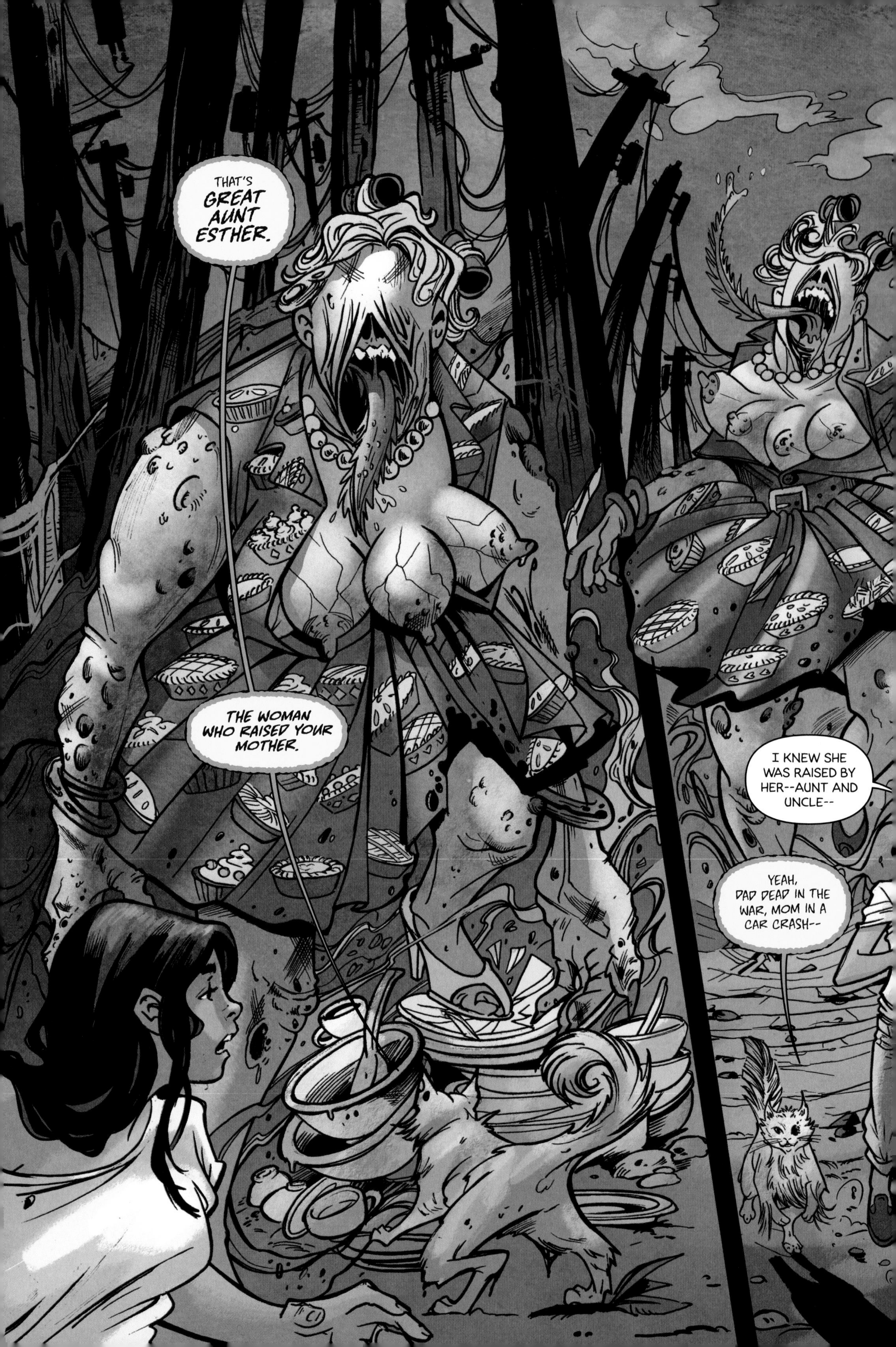
THAT'S GREAT AUNT ESTHER.
THE WOMAN WHO RAISED YOUR MOTHER.
I KNEW SHE WAS RAISED BY HER--AUNT AND UNCLE--
YEAH, DAD DEAD IN THE WAR, MOM IN A CAR CRASH--

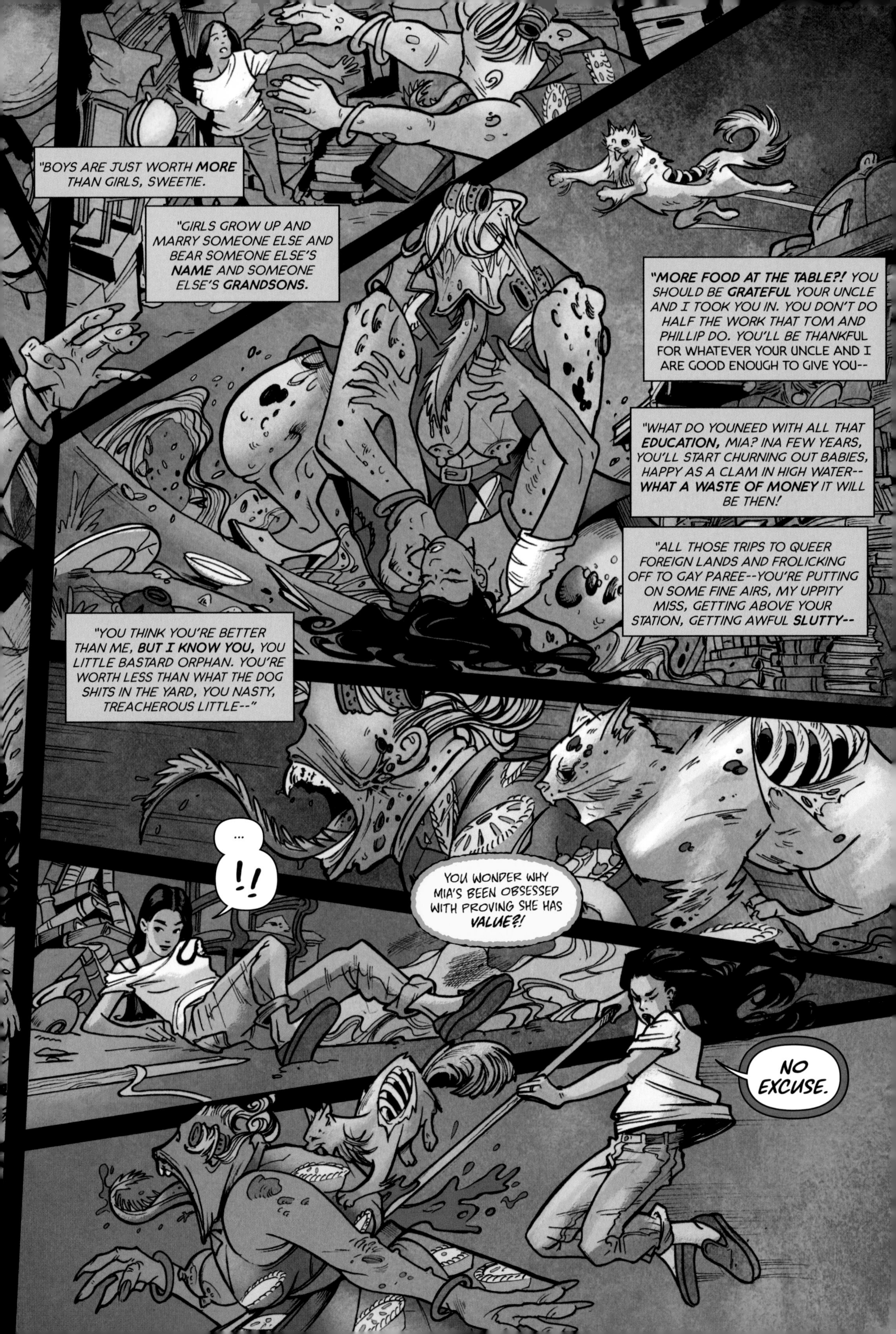
"BOYS ARE JUST WORTH MORE THAN GIRLS, SWEETIE.
"GIRLS GROW UP AND MARRY SOMEONE ELSE AND BEAR SOMEONE ELSE'S NAME AND SOMEONE ELSE'S GRANDSONS.
"MORE FOOD AT THE TABLE?! YOU SHOULD BE GRATEFUL YOUR UNCLE AND I TOOK YOU IN. YOU DON'T DO HALF THE WORK THAT TOM AND PHILLIP DO. YOU'LL BE THANKFUL FOR WHATEVER YOUR UNCLE AND I ARE GOOD ENOUGH TO GIVE YOU--
"WHAT DO YOUNEED WITH ALL THAT EDUCATION, MIA? INA FEW YEARS, YOU'LL START CHURNING OUT BABIES, HAPPY AS A CLAM IN HIGH WATER-- WHAT A WASTE OF MONEY IT WILL BE THEN!
"ALL THOSE TRIPS TO QUEER FOREIGN LANDS AND FROLICKING OFF TO GAY PAREE--YOU'RE PUTTING ON SOME FINE AIRS, MY UPPITY MISS, GETTING ABOVE YOUR STATION, GETTING AWFUL SLUTTY--
"YOU THINK YOU'RE BETTER THAN ME, BUT I KNOW YOU, YOU LITTLE BASTARD ORPHAN. YOU'RE WORTH LESS THAN WHAT THE DOG SHITS IN THE YARD, YOU NASTY, TREACHEROUS LITTLE--"
...
!!
YOU WONDER WHY MIA'S BEEN OBSESSED WITH PROVING SHE HAS VALUE?!
NO EXCUSE.

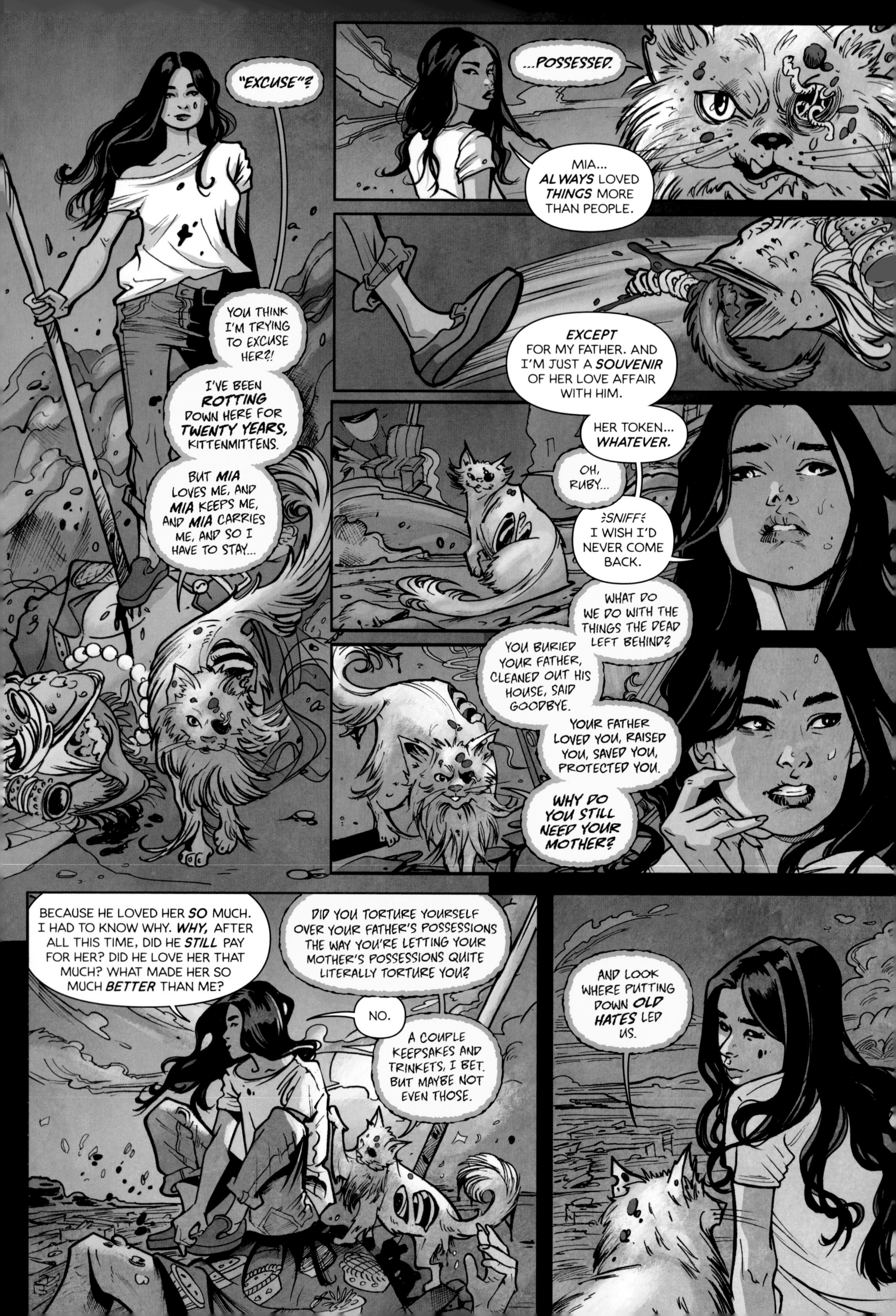
"EXCUSE"?
YOU THINK I'M TRYING TO EXCUSE HER?!
I'VE BEEN ROTTING DOWN HERE FOR TWENTY YEARS, KITTENMITTENS.
BUT MIA LOVES ME, AND MIA KEEPS ME, AND MIA CARRIES ME, AND SO I HAVE TO STAY...
...POSSESSED.
MIA... ALWAYS LOVED THINGS MORE THAN PEOPLE.
EXCEPT FOR MY FATHER. AND I'M JUST A SOUVENIR OF HER LOVE AFFAIR WITH HIM.
HER TOKEN... WHATEVER.
OH, RUBY...
SNIFF
I WISH I'D NEVER COME BACK.
WHAT DO WE DO WITH THE THINGS THE DEAD LEFT BEHIND?
YOU BURIED YOUR FATHER, CLEANED OUT HIS HOUSE, SAID GOODBYE.
YOUR FATHER LOVED YOU, RAISED YOU, SAVED YOU, PROTECTED YOU.
WHY DO YOU STILL NEED YOUR MOTHER?
BECAUSE HE LOVED HER SO MUCH. I HAD TO KNOW WHY. WHY, AFTER ALL THIS TIME, DID HE STILL PAY FOR HER? DID HE LOVE HER THAT MUCH? WHAT MADE HER SO MUCH BETTER THAN ME?
DID YOU TORTURE YOURSELF OVER YOUR FATHER'S POSSESSIONS THE WAY YOU'RE LETTING YOUR MOTHER'S POSSESSIONS QUITE LITERALLY TORTURE YOU?
NO.
A COUPLE KEEPSAKES AND TRINKETS, I BET. BUT MAYBE NOT EVEN THOSE.
AND LOOK WHERE PUTTING DOWN OLD HATES LED US.

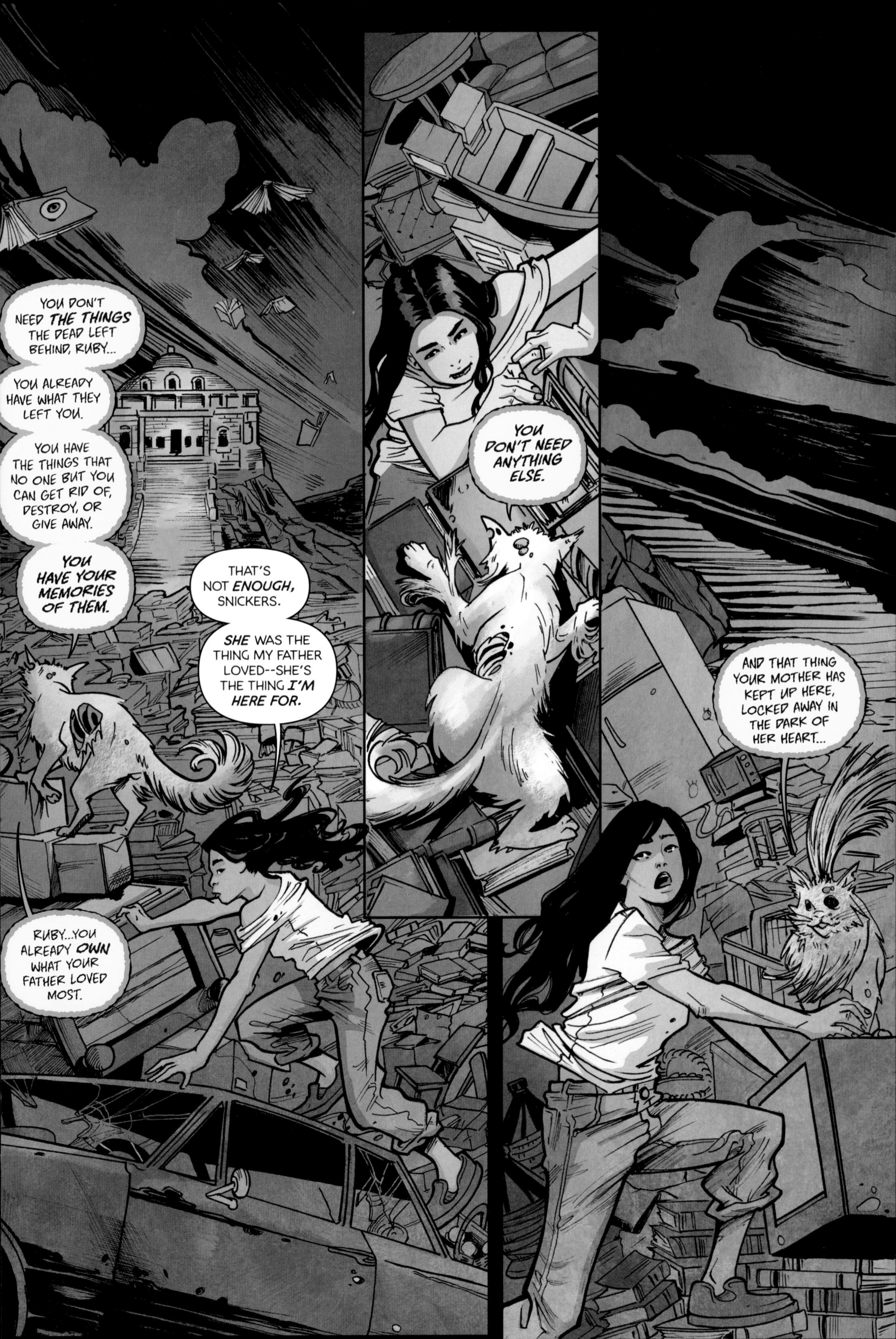
YOU DON'T NEED THE THINGS THE DEAD LEFT BEHIND, RUBY...
YOU ALREADY HAVE WHAT THEY LEFT YOU.
YOU HAVE THE THINGS THAT NO ONE BUT YOU CAN GET RID OF, DESTROY, OR GIVE AWAY.
YOU HAVE YOUR MEMORIES OF THEM.
THAT'S NOT ENOUGH, SNICKERS.
SHE WAS THE THING MY FATHER LOVED--SHE'S THE THING I'M HERE FOR.
RUBY...YOU ALREADY OWN WHAT YOUR FATHER LOVED MOST.
YOU DON'T NEED ANYTHING ELSE.
AND THAT THING YOUR MOTHER HAS KEPT UP HERE, LOCKED AWAY IN THE DARK OF HER HEART...

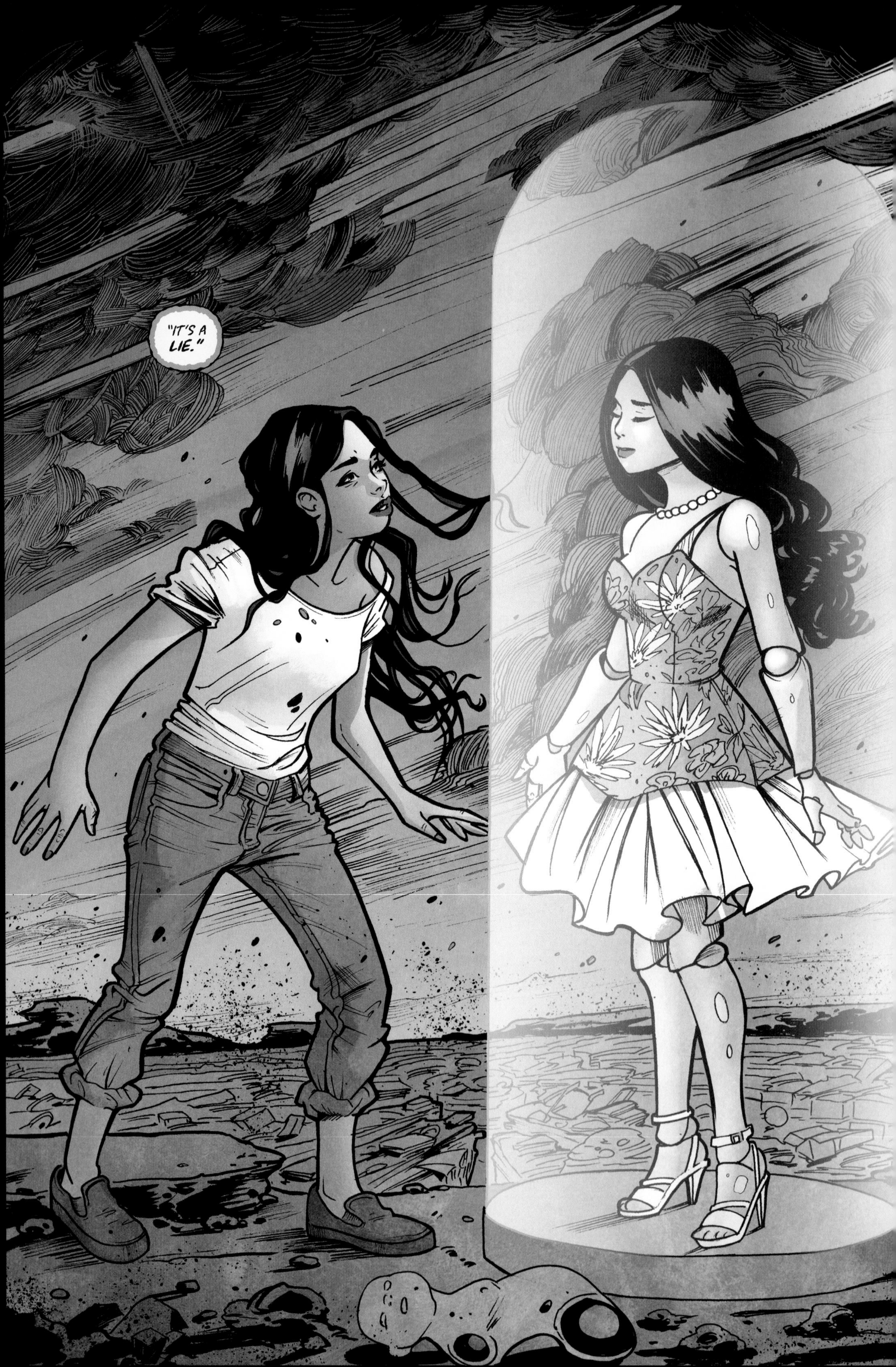
"IT'S A LIE."

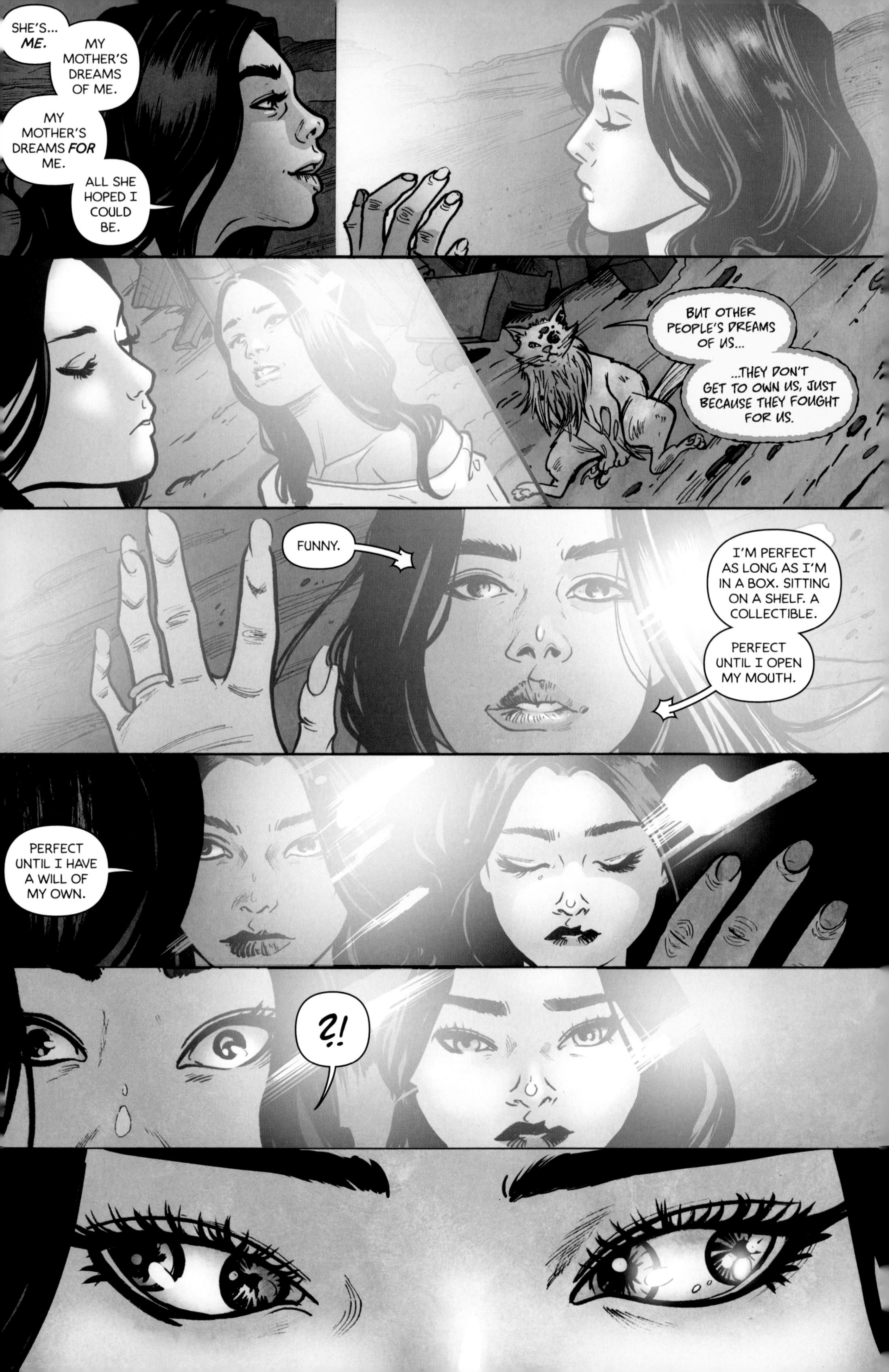
SHE'S... ME.
MY MOTHER'S DREAMS OF ME.
MY MOTHER'S DREAMS FOR ME.
ALL SHE HOPED I COULD BE.
BUT OTHER PEOPLE'S DREAMS OF US...
...THEY DON'T GET TO OWN US, JUST BECAUSE THEY FOUGHT FOR US.
FUNNY.
I'M PERFECT AS LONG AS I'M IN A BOX. SITTING ON A SHELF. A COLLECTIBLE.
PERFECT UNTIL I OPEN MY MOUTH.
PERFECT UNTIL I HAVE A WILL OF MY OWN.
?!

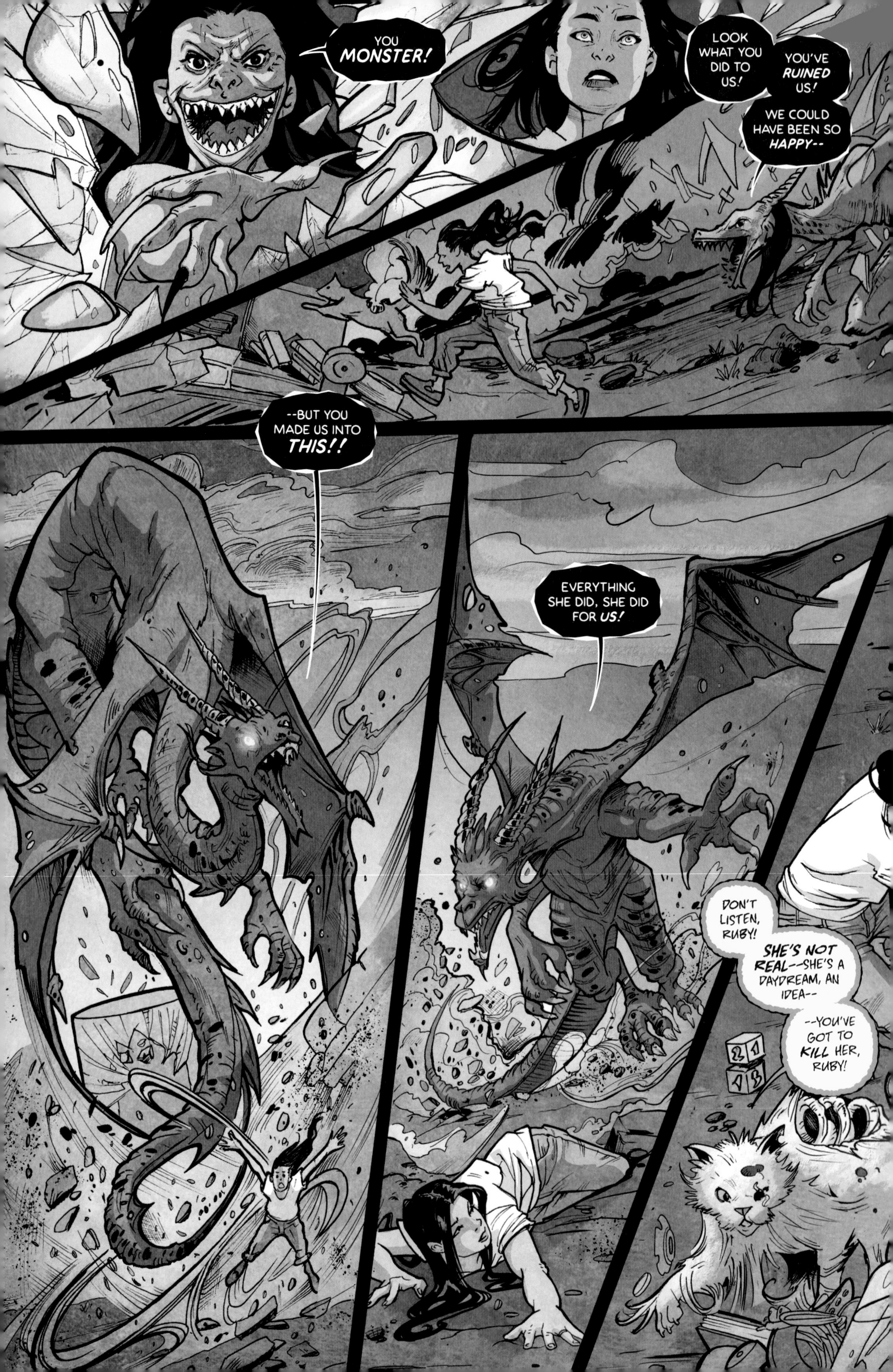
YOU MONSTER!
LOOK WHAT YOU DID TO US!
YOU'VE RUINED US!
WE COULD HAVE BEEN SO HAPPY--
--BUT YOU MADE US INTO THIS!!
EVERYTHING SHE DID, SHE DID FOR US!
DON'T LISTEN, RUBY!
SHE'S NOT REAL--SHE'S A DAYDREAM, AN IDEA--
--YOU'VE GOT TO KILL HER, RUBY!

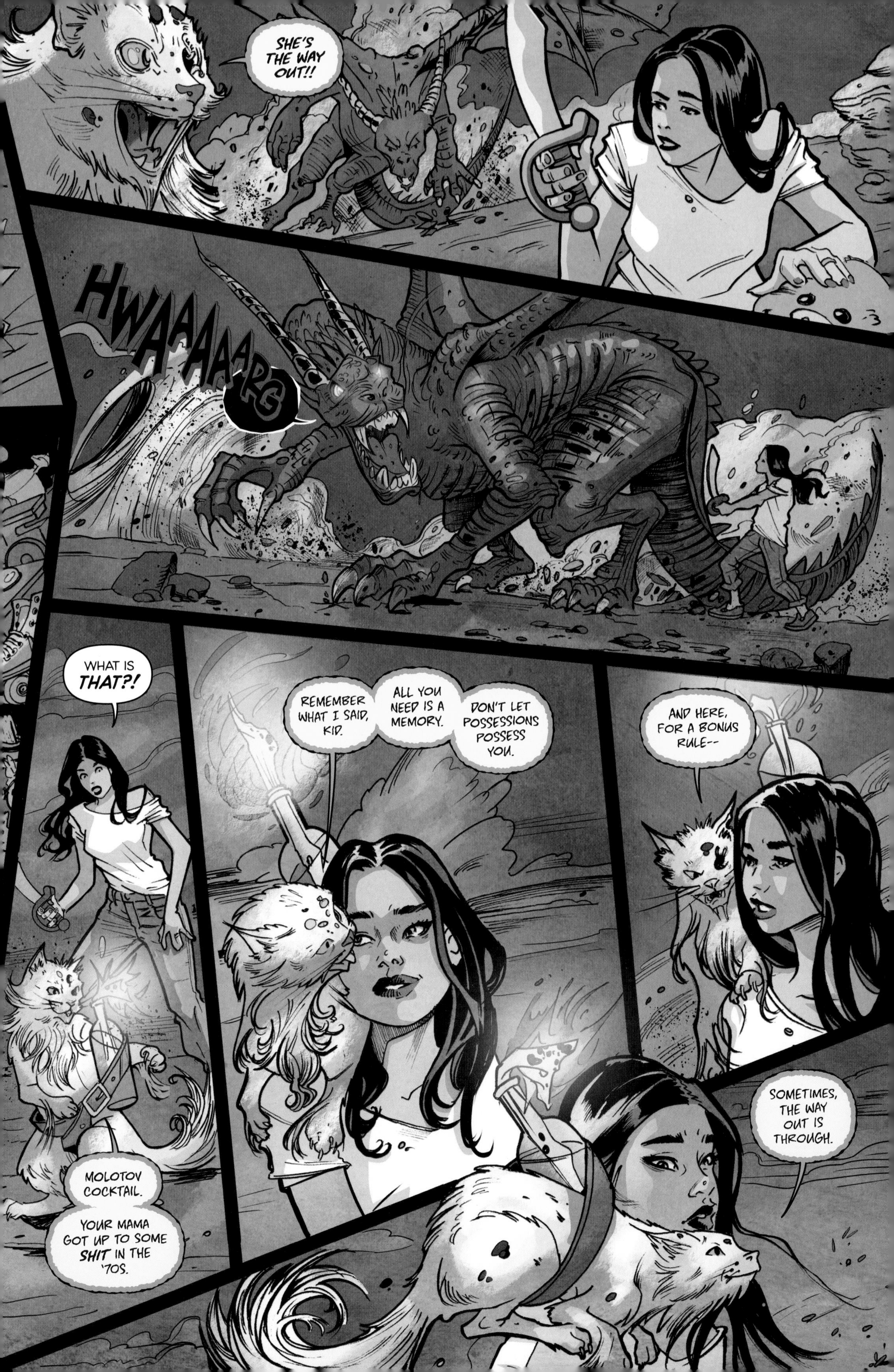
SHE'S THE WAY OUT!!
HWAAAAAARG
WHAT IS THAT?!
MOLOTOV COCKTAIL.
YOUR MAMA GOT UP TO SOME SHIT IN THE '70S.
REMEMBER WHAT I SAID, KID.
ALL YOU NEED IS A MEMORY.
DON'T LET POSSESSIONS POSSESS YOU.
AND HERE, FOR A BONUS RULE--
SOMETIMES, THE WAY OUT IS THROUGH.

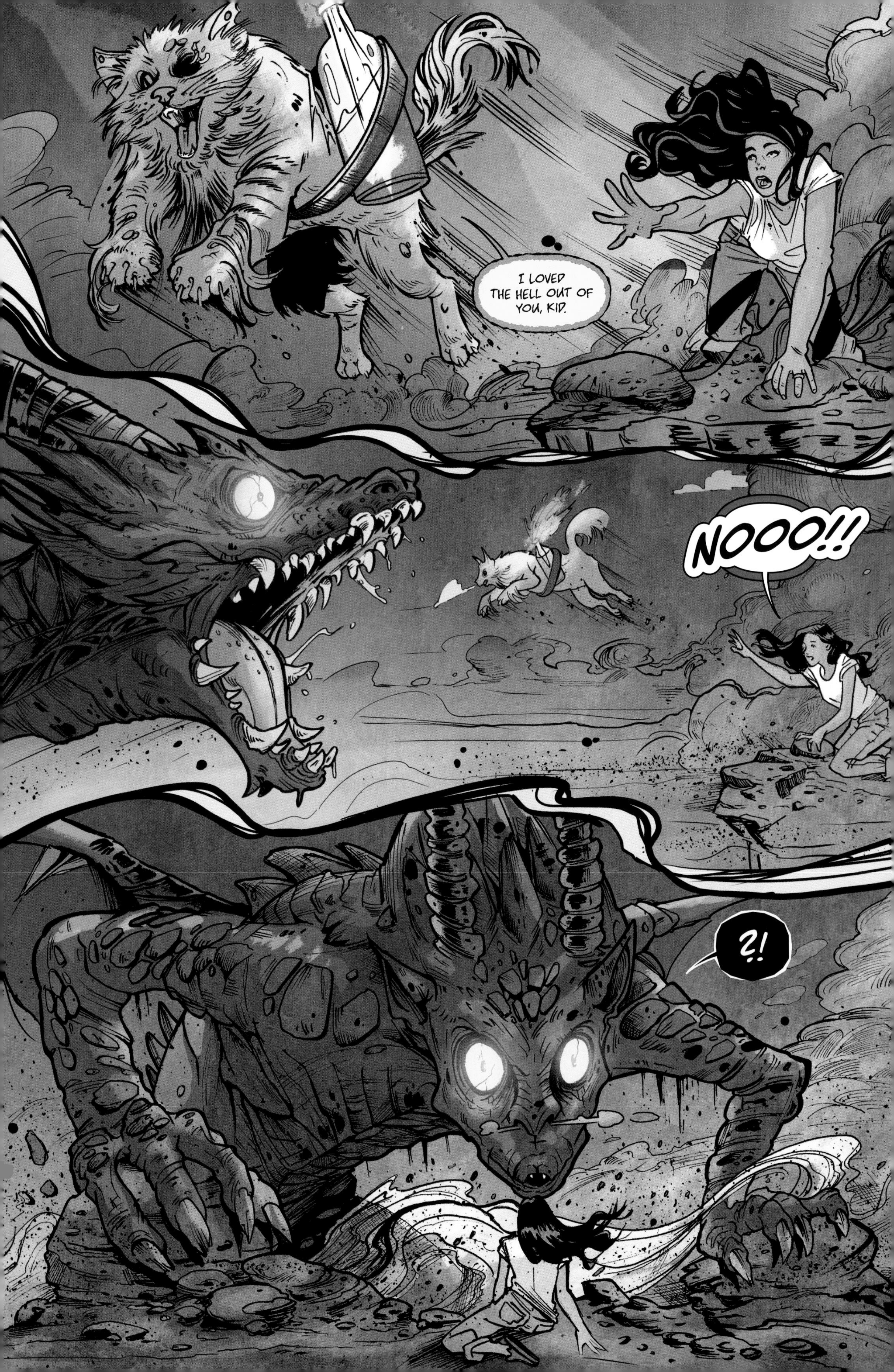
I LOVED THE HELL OUT OF YOU, KID.
NOOO!!
?!

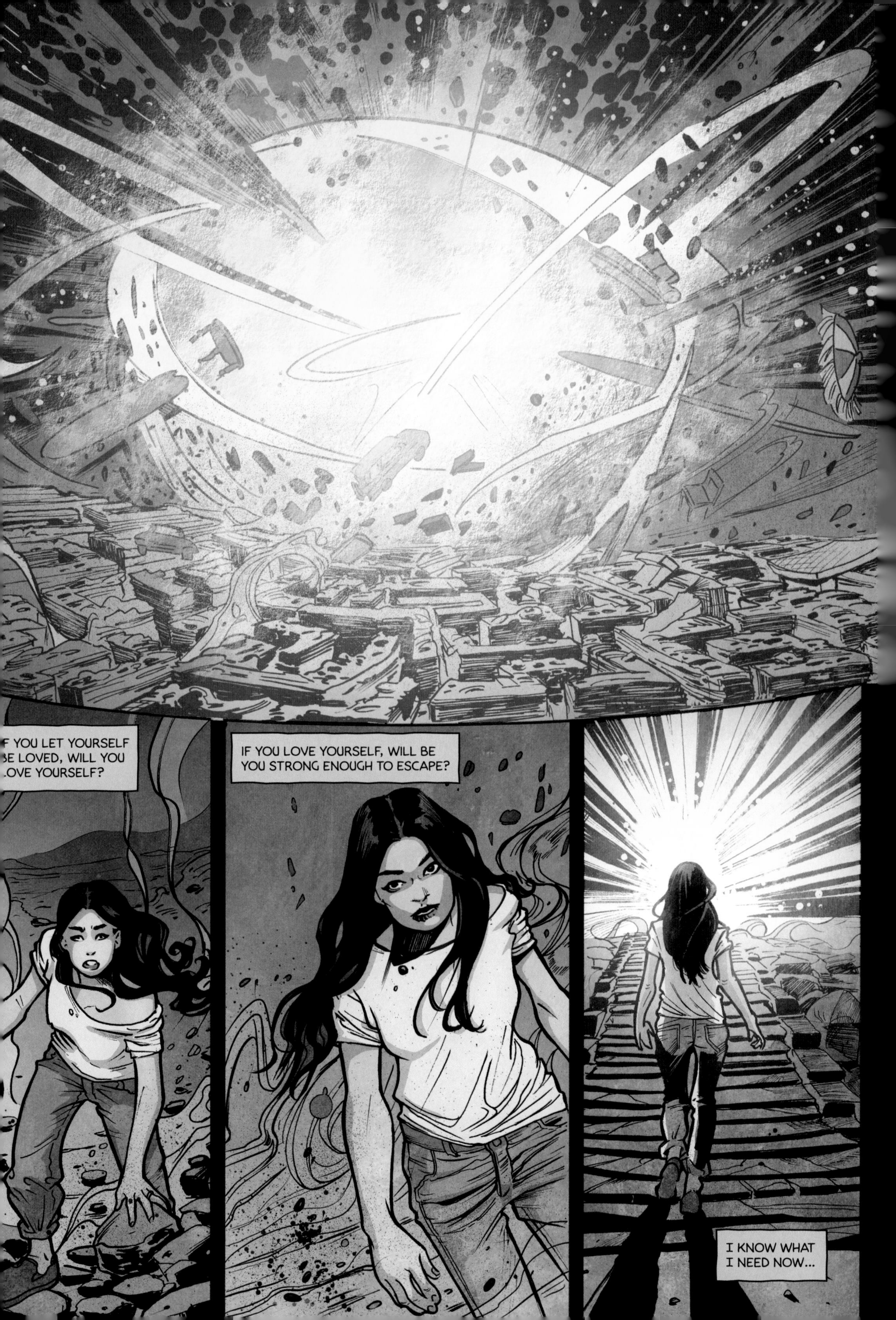

F YOU LET YOURSELF
BE LOVED, WILL YOU
LOVE YOURSELF?
IF YOU LOVE YOURSELF, WILL BE YOU STRONG ENOUGH TO ESCAPE?
I KNOW WHAT I NEED NOW...

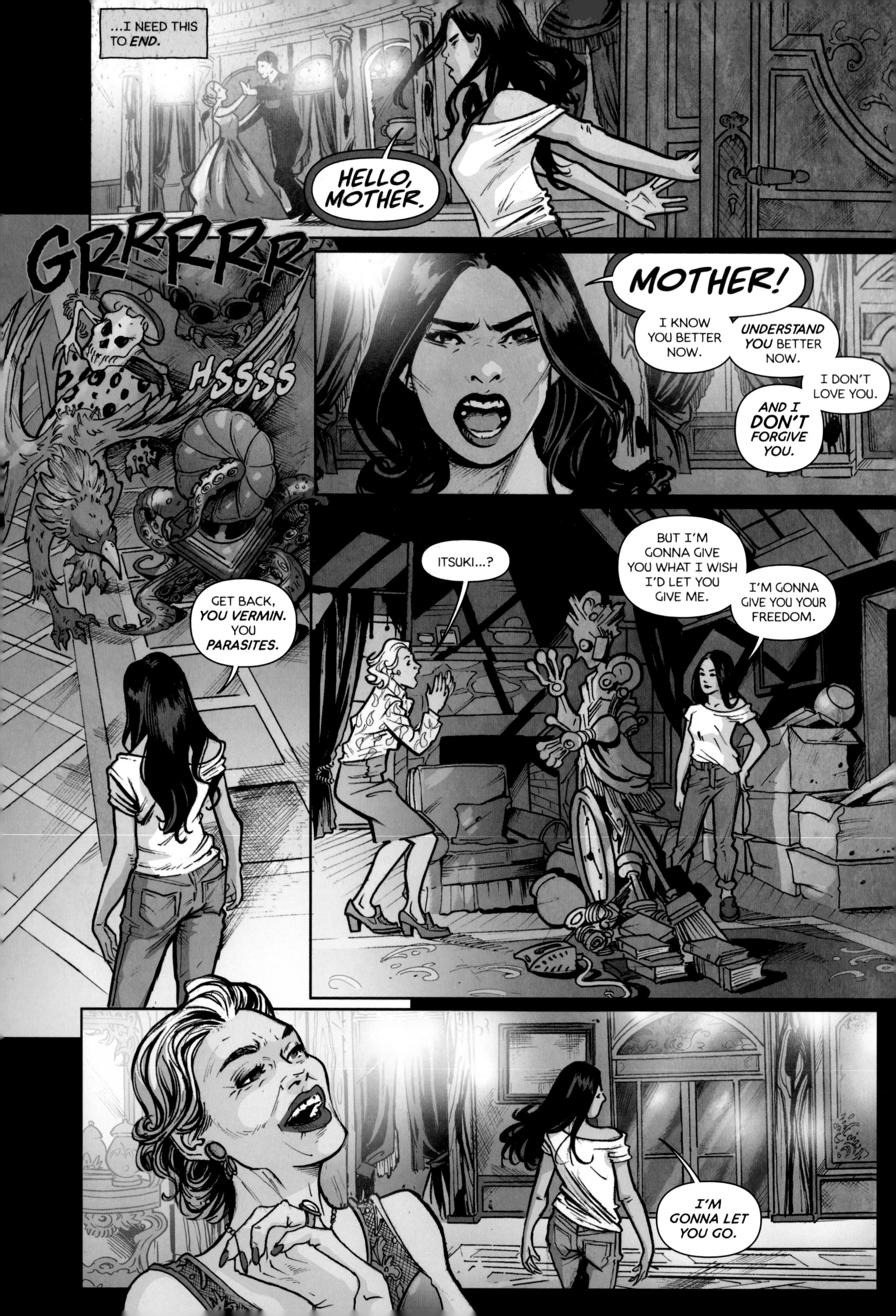
...I NEED THIS TO END.
HELLO, MOTHER.
GRRRRRR
HSSSS
MOTHER!
I KNOW YOU BETTER NOW.
UNDERSTAND YOU BETTER NOW.
I DON'T LOVE YOU.
AND I DON'T FORGIVE YOU.
GET BACK, YOU VERMIN. YOU PARASITES.
ITSUKI...?
BUT I'M GONNA GIVE YOU WHAT I WISH I'D LET YOU GIVE ME.
I'M GONNA GIVE YOU YOUR FREEDOM.
I'M GONNA LET YOU GO.

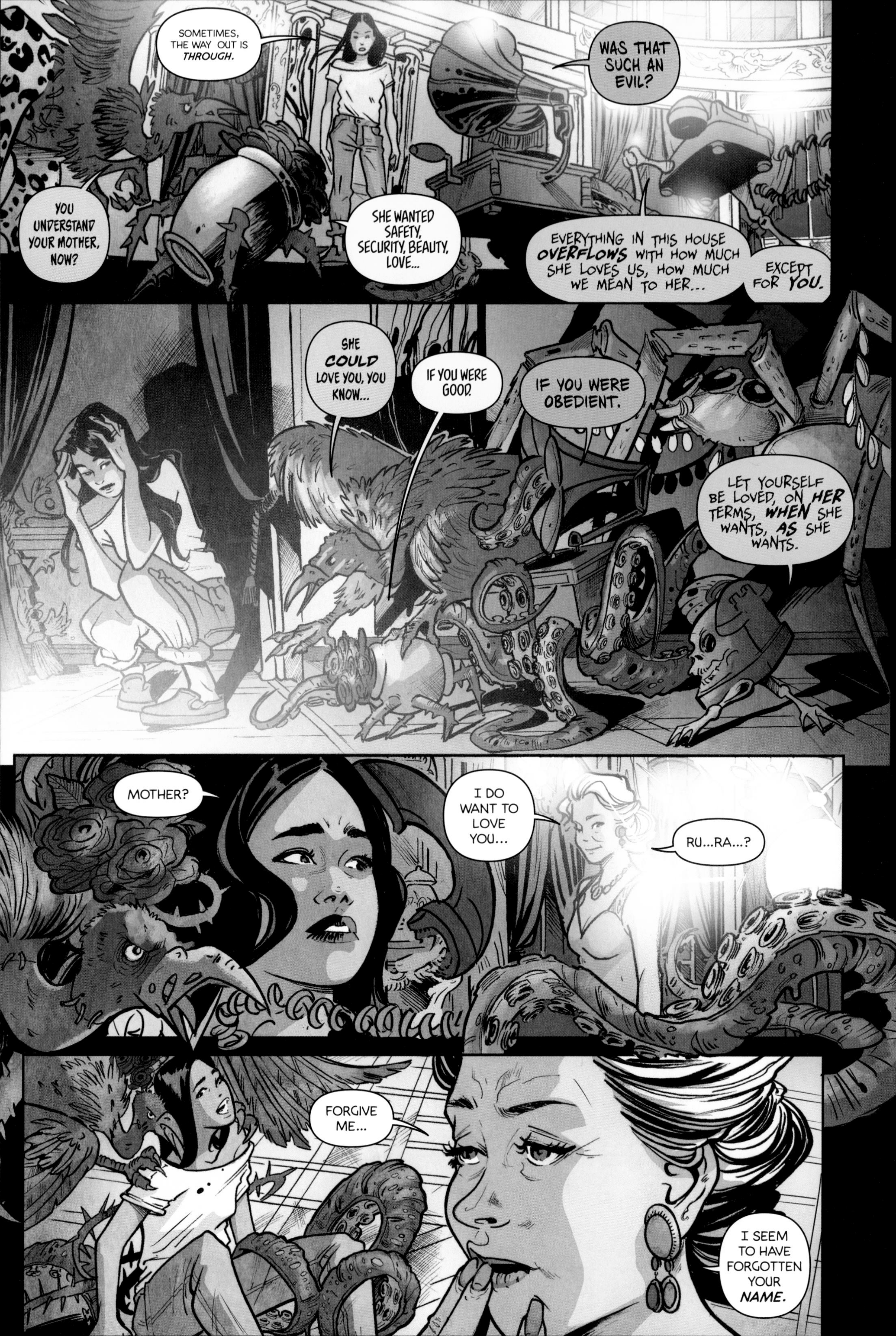

SOMETIMES, THE WAY OUT IS THROUGH.
WAS THAT SUCH AN EVIL?
YOU UNDERSTAND YOUR MOTHER, NOW?
SHE WANTED SAFETY, SECURITY, BEAUTY, LOVE...
EVERYTHING IN THIS HOUSE OVERFLOWS WITH HOW MUCH SHE LOVES US, HOW MUCH WE MEAN TO HER...
EXCEPT FOR YOU.
SHE COULD LOVE YOU, YOU KNOW...
IF YOU WERE GOOD.
IF YOU WERE OBEDIENT.
LET YOURSELF BE LOVED, ON HER TERMS, WHEN SHE WANTS, AS SHE WANTS.
MOTHER?
I DO WANT TO LOVE YOU...
RU...RA...?
FORGIVE ME...
I SEEM TO HAVE FORGOTTEN YOUR NAME.

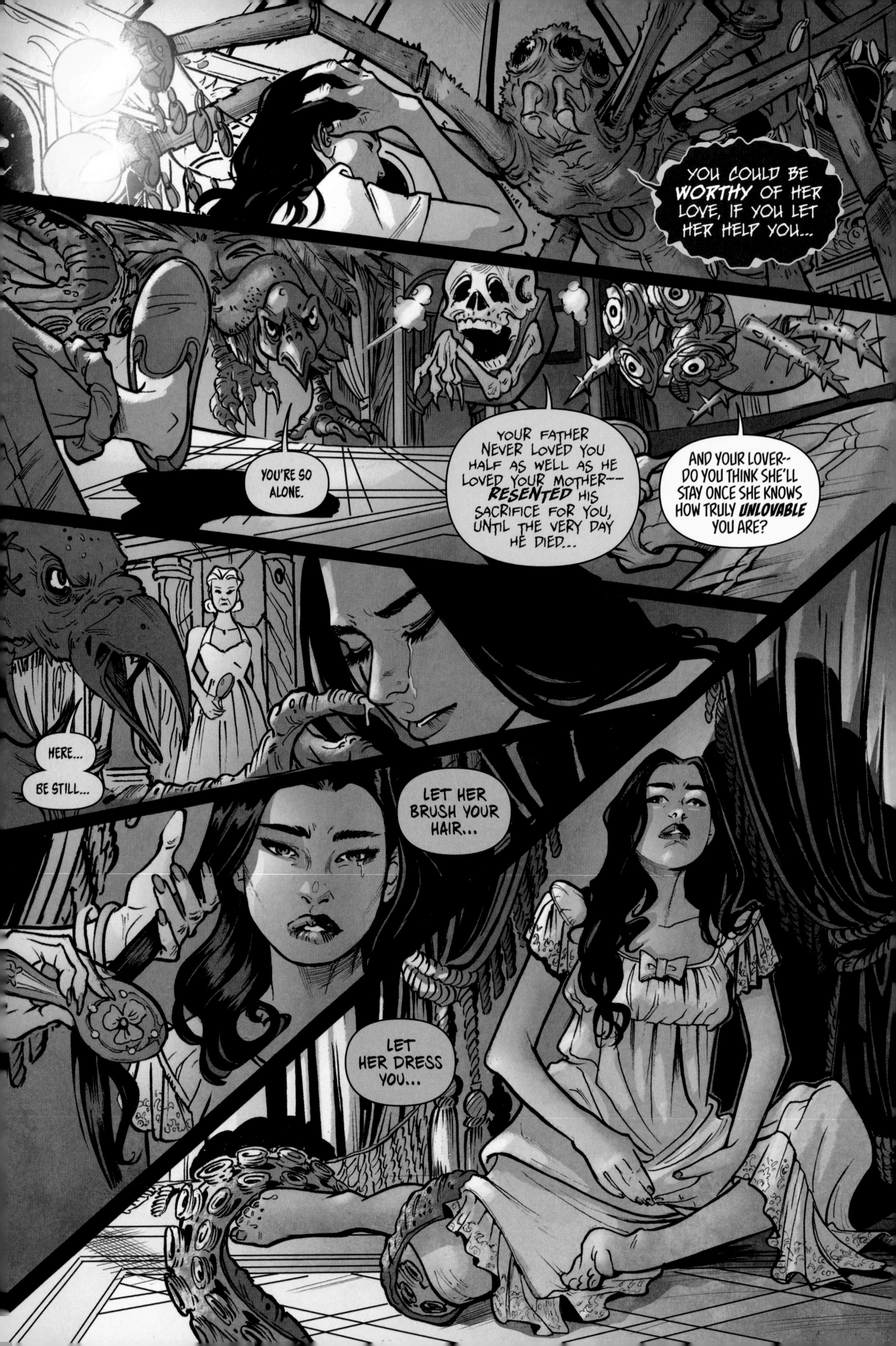
YOU COULD BE WORTHY OF HER LOVE, IF YOU LET HER HELP YOU...
YOU'RE SO ALONE.
YOUR FATHER NEVER LOVED YOU HALF AS WELL AS HE LOVED YOUR MOTHER-- RESENTED HIS SACRIFICE FOR YOU, UNTIL THE VERY DAY HE DIED...
AND YOUR LOVER-- DO YOU THINK SHE'LL STAY ONCE SHE KNOWS HOW TRULY UNLOVABLE YOU ARE?
HERE...
BE STILL...
LET HER BRUSH YOUR HAIR...
LET HER DRESS YOU...

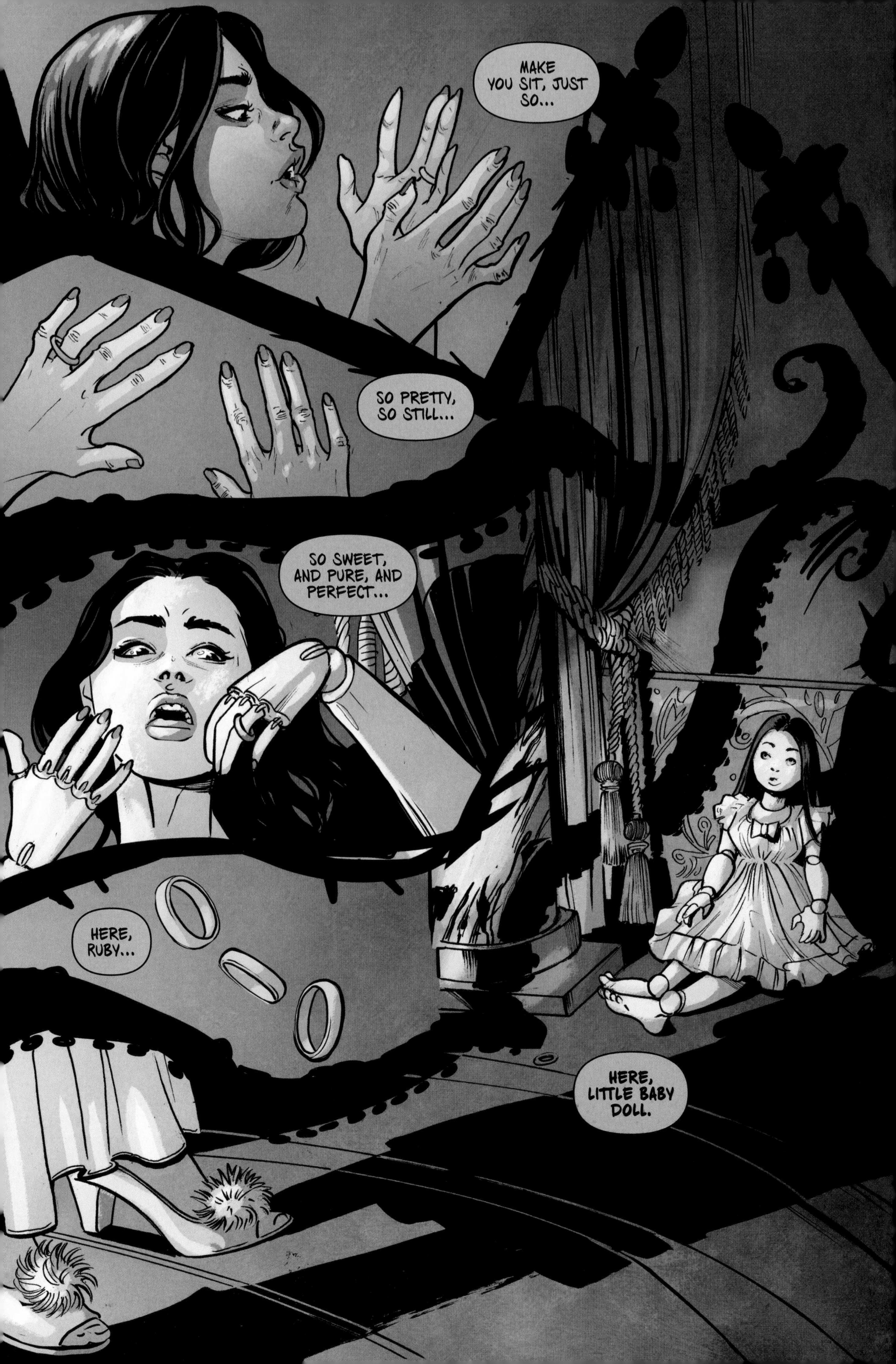
MAKE YOU SIT, JUST SO...
SO PRETTY, SO STILL...
SO SWEET, AND PURE, AND PERFECT...
HERE, RUBY...
HERE, LITTLE BABY DOLL.

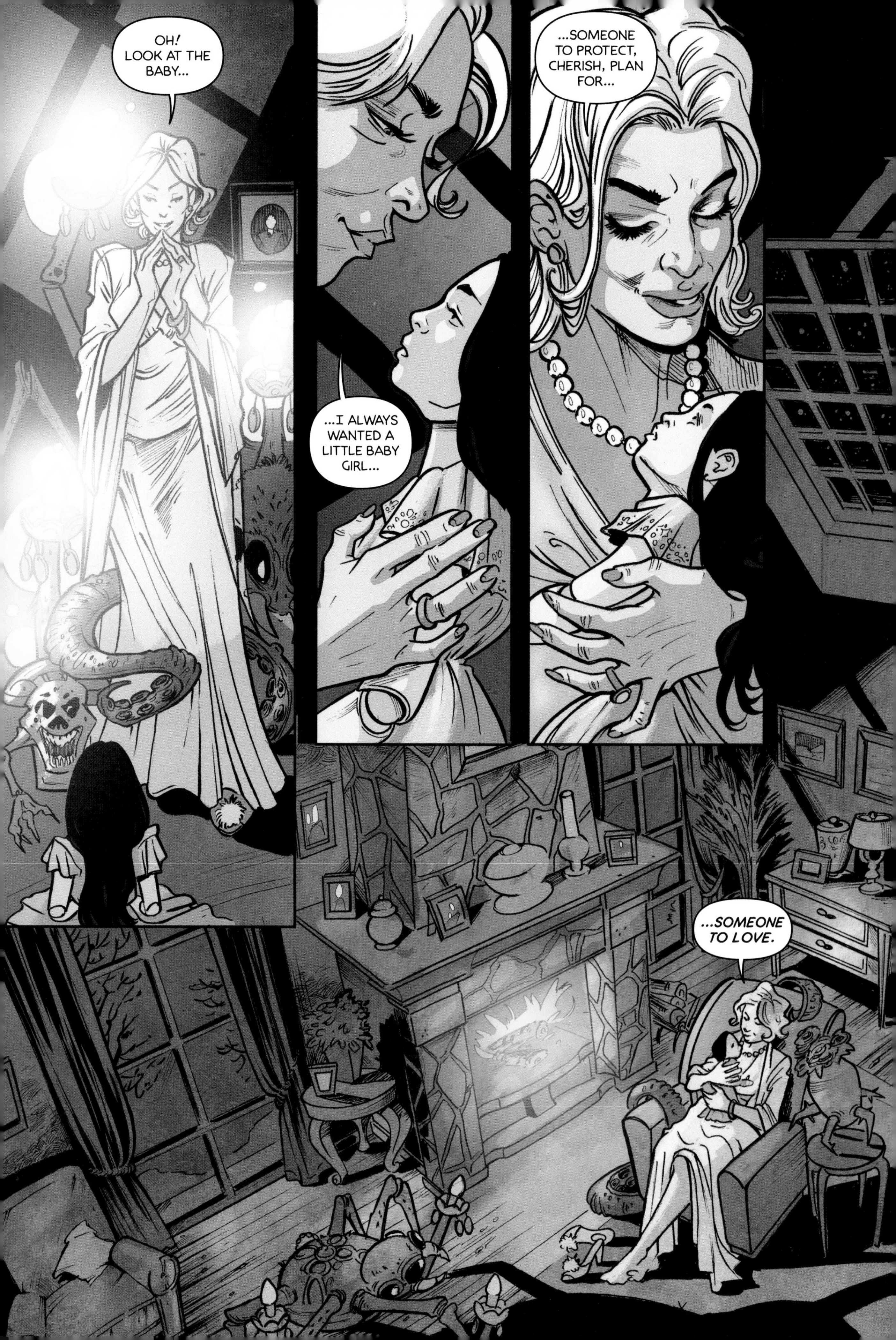
OH! LOOK AT THE BABY...
...I ALWAYS WANTED A LITTLE BABY GIRL...
...SOMEONE TO PROTECT, CHERISH, PLAN FOR...
...SOMEONE TO LOVE.

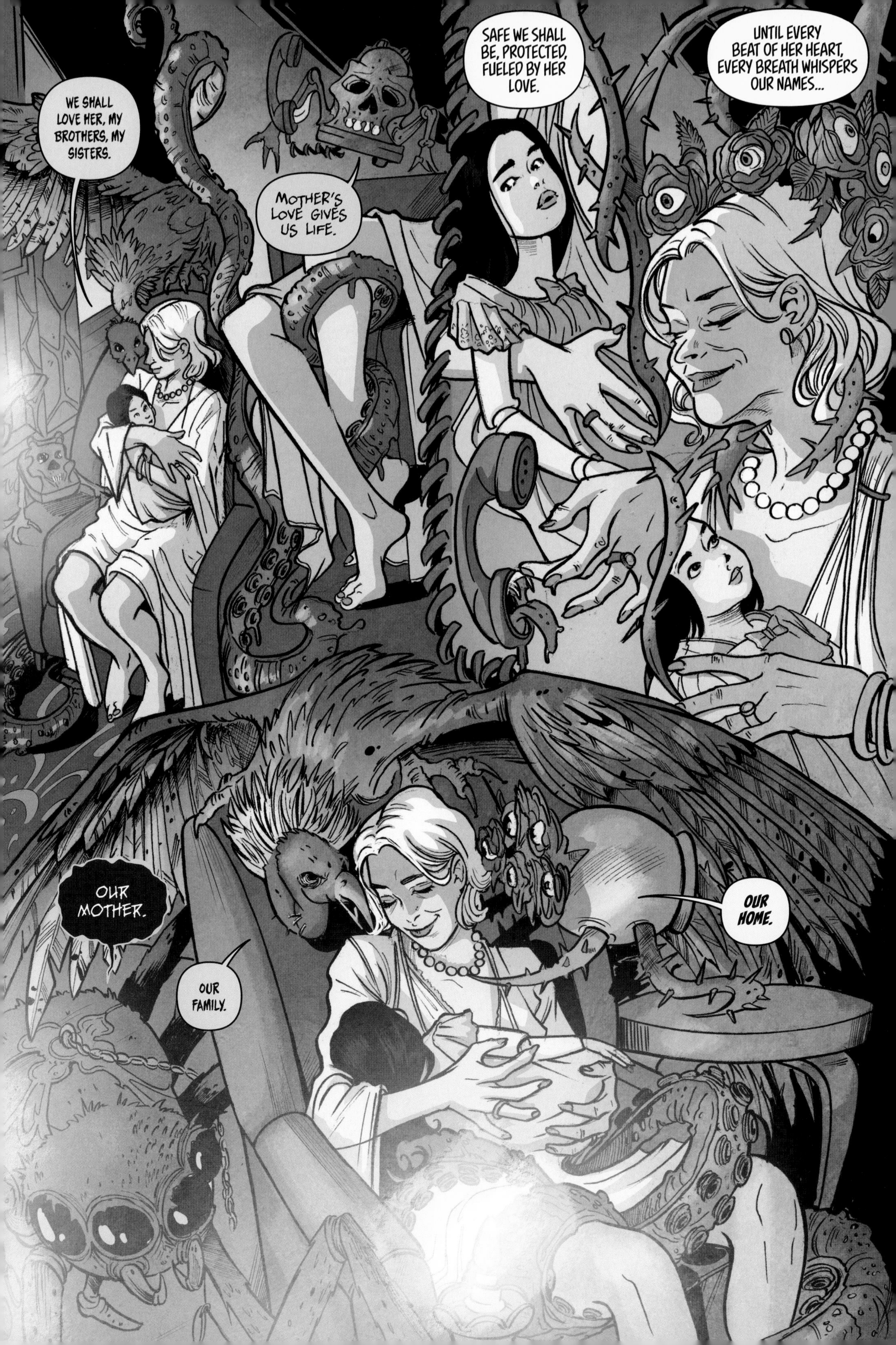
WE SHALL LOVE HER, MY BROTHERS, MY SISTERS.
MOTHER'S LOVE GIVES US LIFE.
SAFE WE SHALL BE, PROTECTED, FUELED BY HER LOVE.
UNTIL EVERY BEAT OF HER HEART, EVERY BREATH WHISPERS OUR NAMES...
OUR MOTHER.
OUR FAMILY.
OUR HOME.

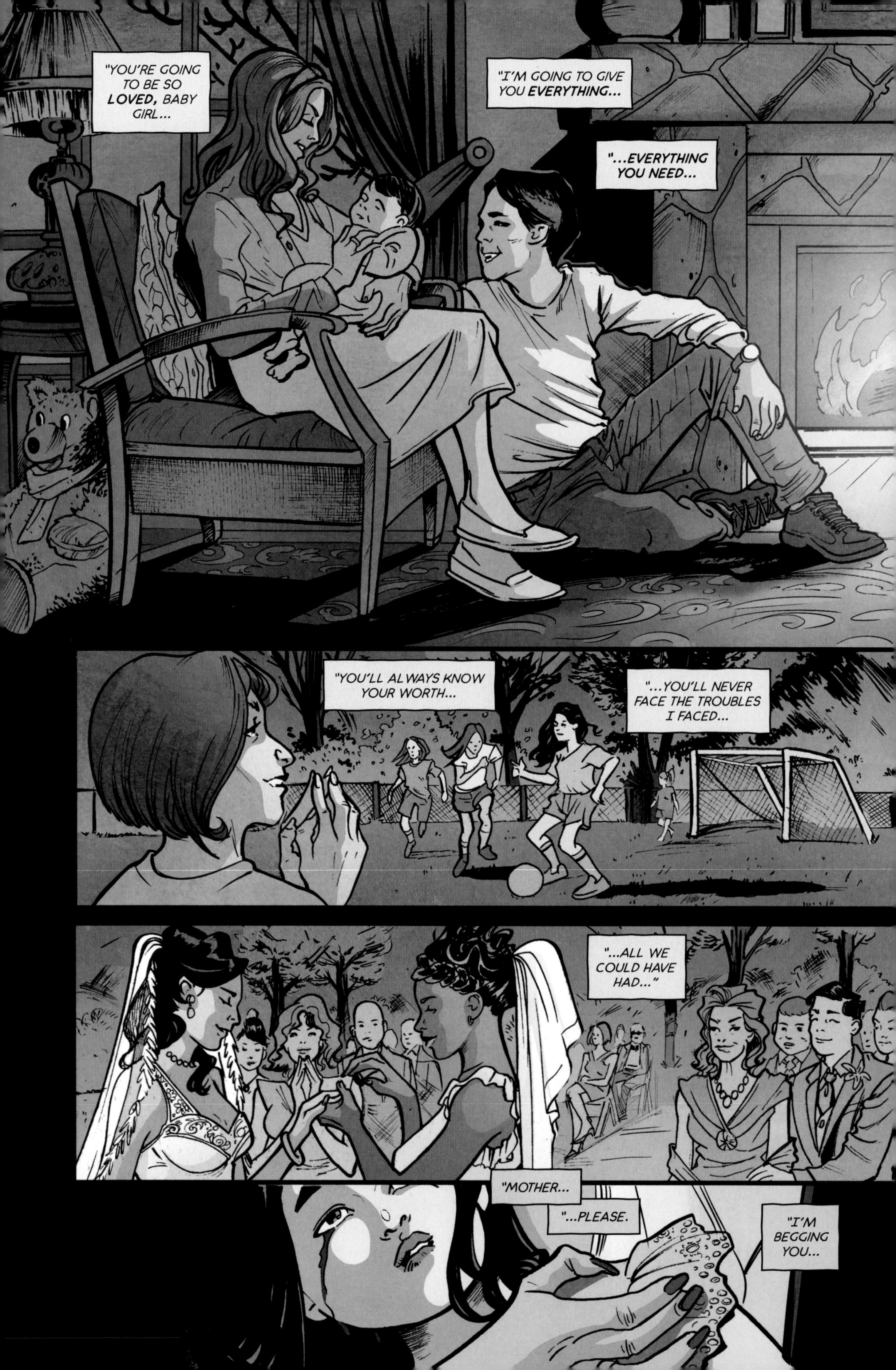
"YOU'RE GOING TO BE SO **LOVED,** BABY GIRL...
"I'M GOING TO GIVE YOU **EVERYTHING...**
"...EVERYTHING YOU NEED...
"YOU'LL ALWAYS KNOW YOUR WORTH...
"...YOU'LL NEVER FACE THE TROUBLES I FACED...
"...ALL WE COULD HAVE HAD..."
"MOTHER...
"...PLEASE.
"I'M BEGGING YOU...

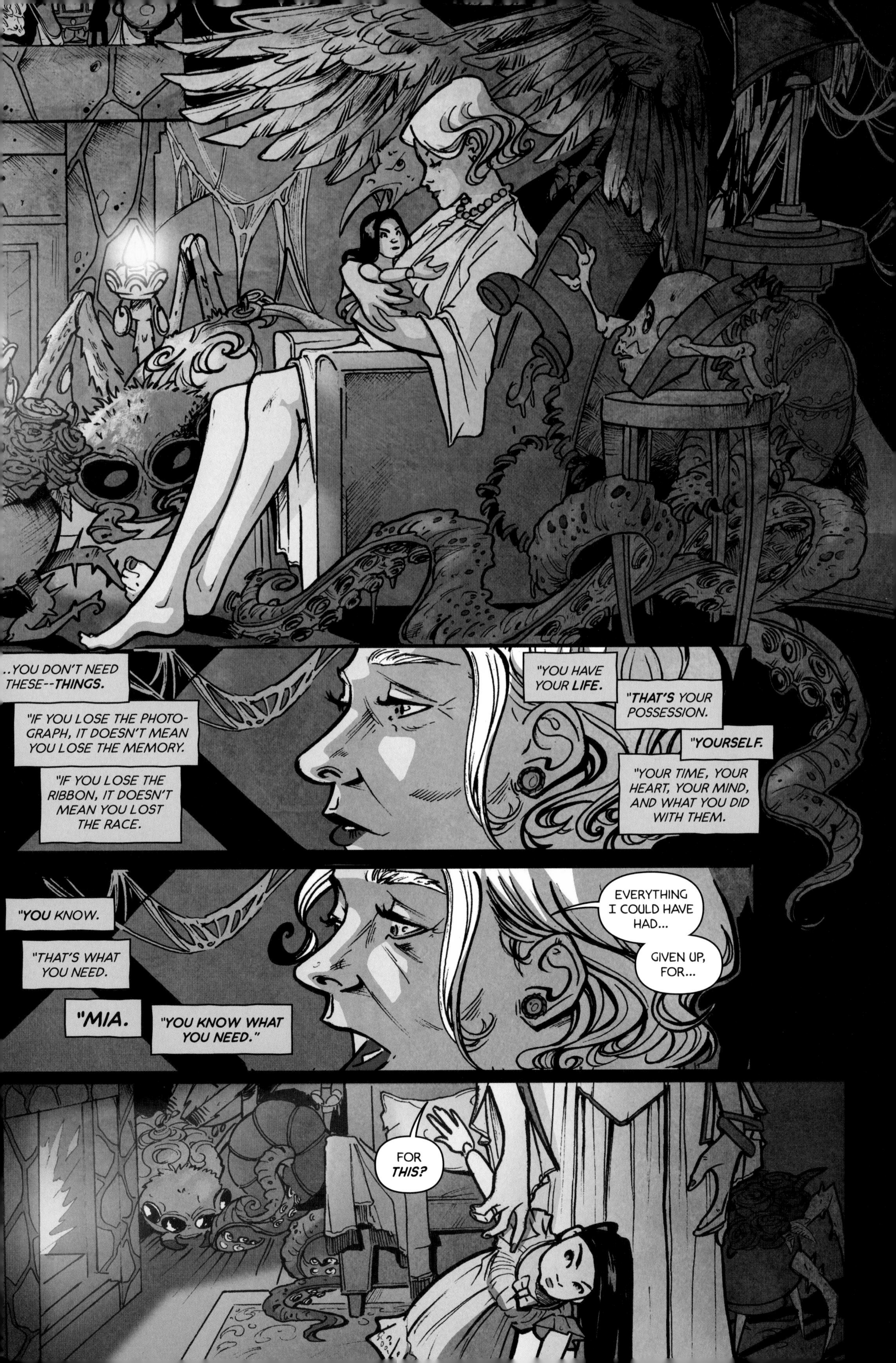
..YOU DON'T NEED THESE--THINGS.
"IF YOU LOSE THE PHOTOGRAPH, IT DOESN'T MEAN YOU LOSE THE MEMORY.
"IF YOU LOSE THE RIBBON, IT DOESN'T MEAN YOU LOST THE RACE.
"YOU HAVE YOUR LIFE.
"THAT'S YOUR POSSESSION.
"YOURSELF.
"YOUR TIME, YOUR HEART, YOUR MIND, AND WHAT YOU DID WITH THEM.
"YOU KNOW.
"THAT'S WHAT YOU NEED.
"MIA.
"YOU KNOW WHAT YOU NEED."
EVERYTHING I COULD HAVE HAD...
GIVEN UP, FOR...
FOR THIS?

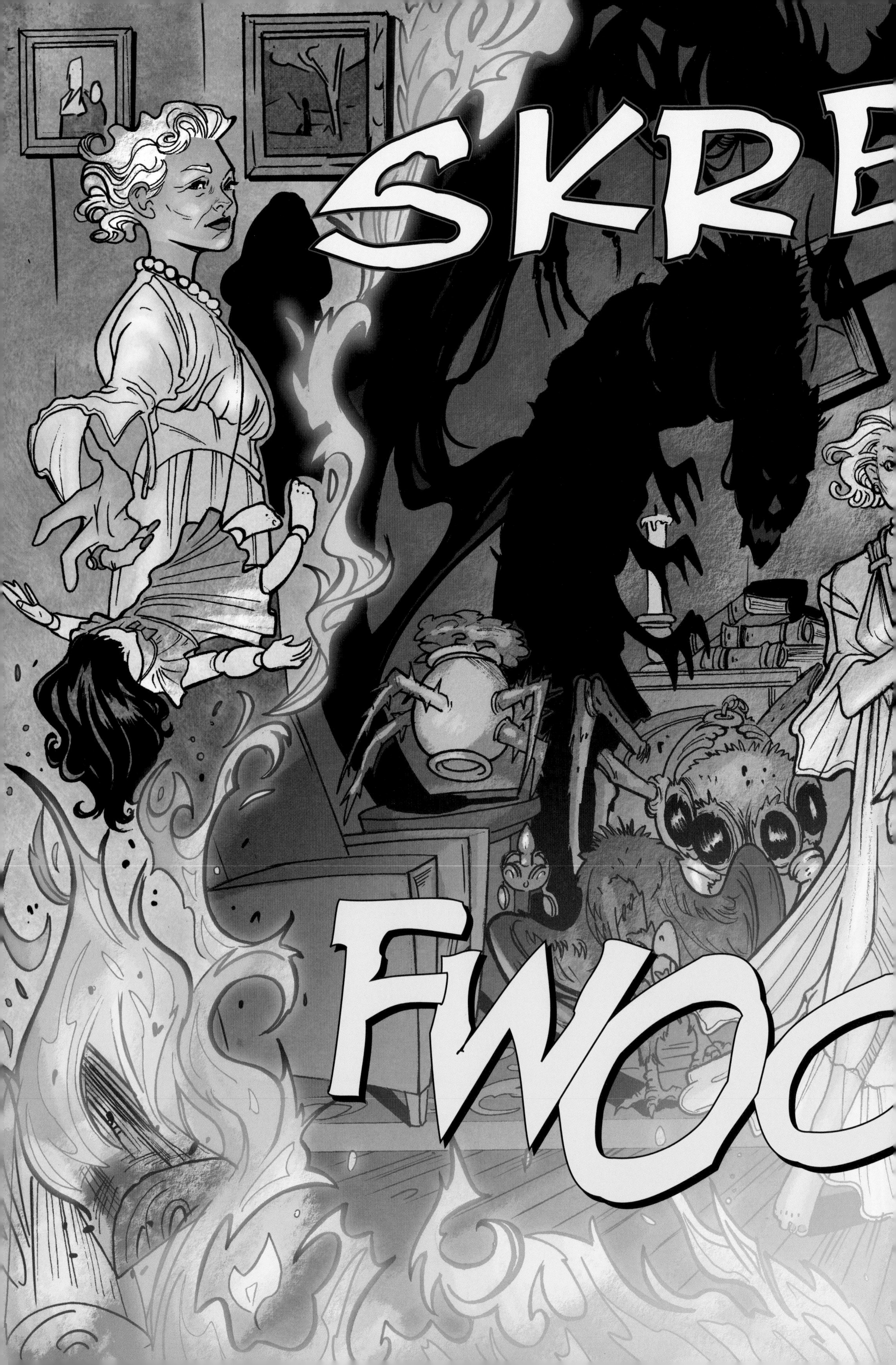
SKRE
FWOO

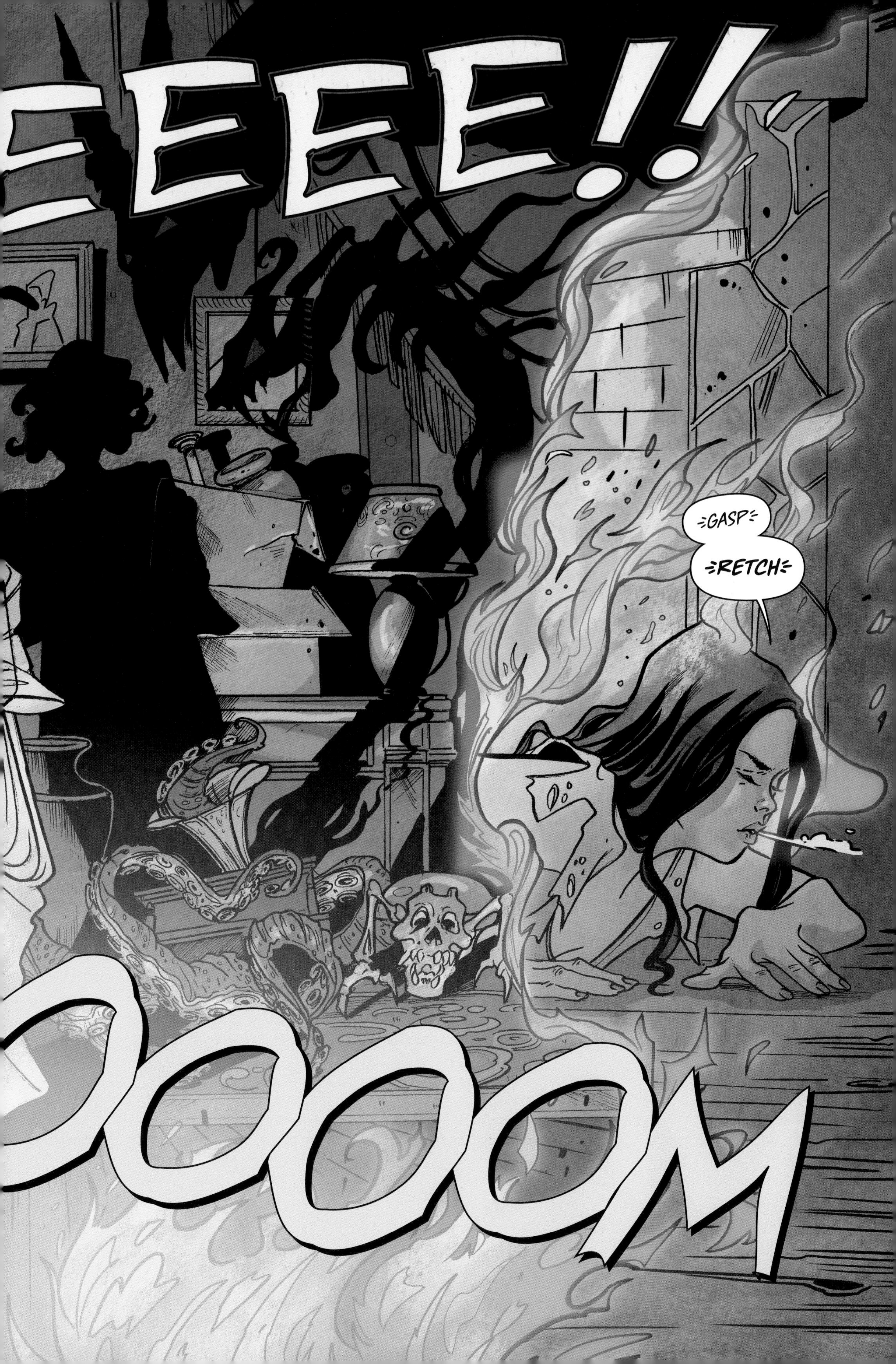
EEEE!!
GASP
RETCH
OOOOM

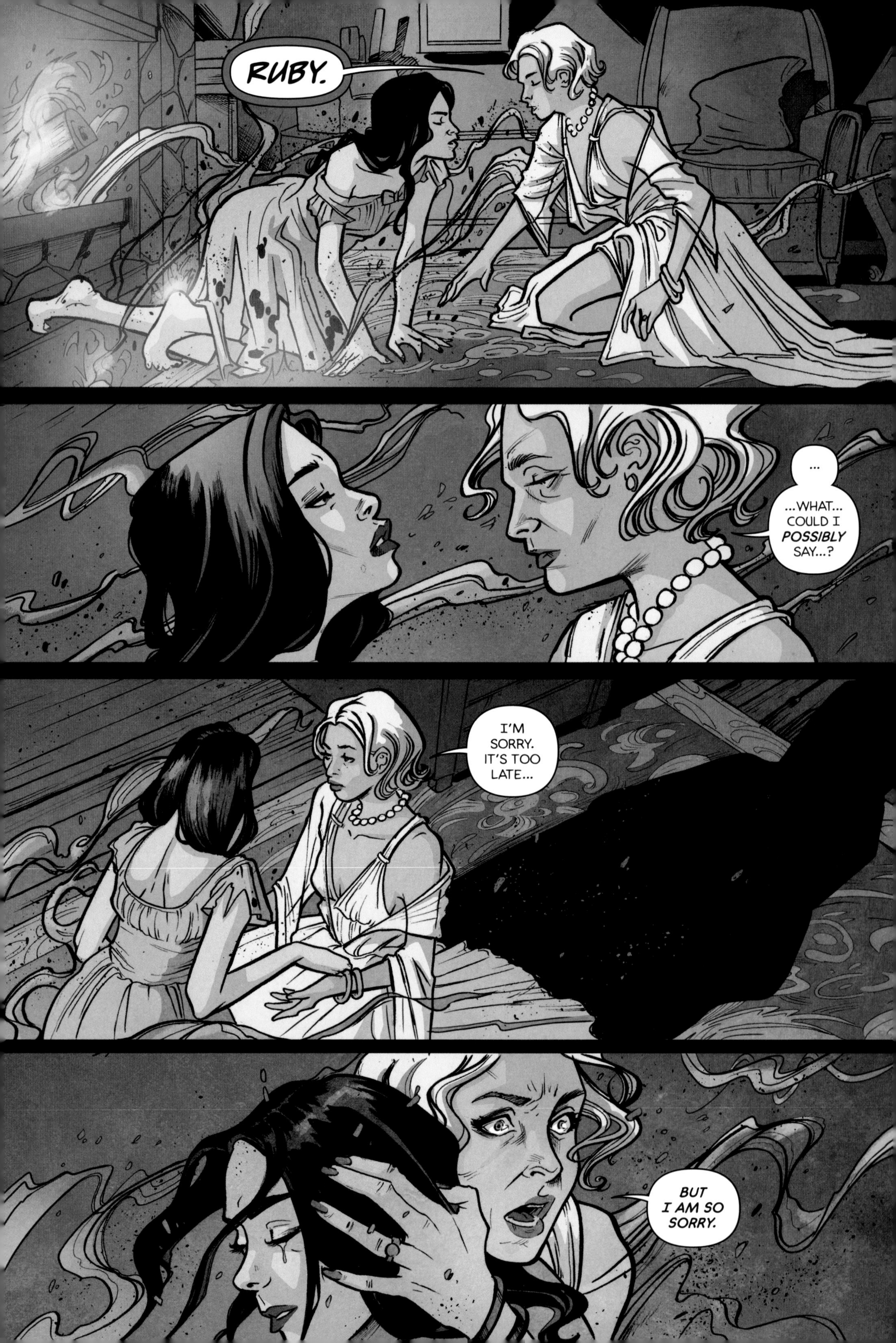
RUBY.
...
...WHAT... COULD I POSSIBLY SAY...?
I'M SORRY. IT'S TOO LATE...
BUT I AM SO SORRY.

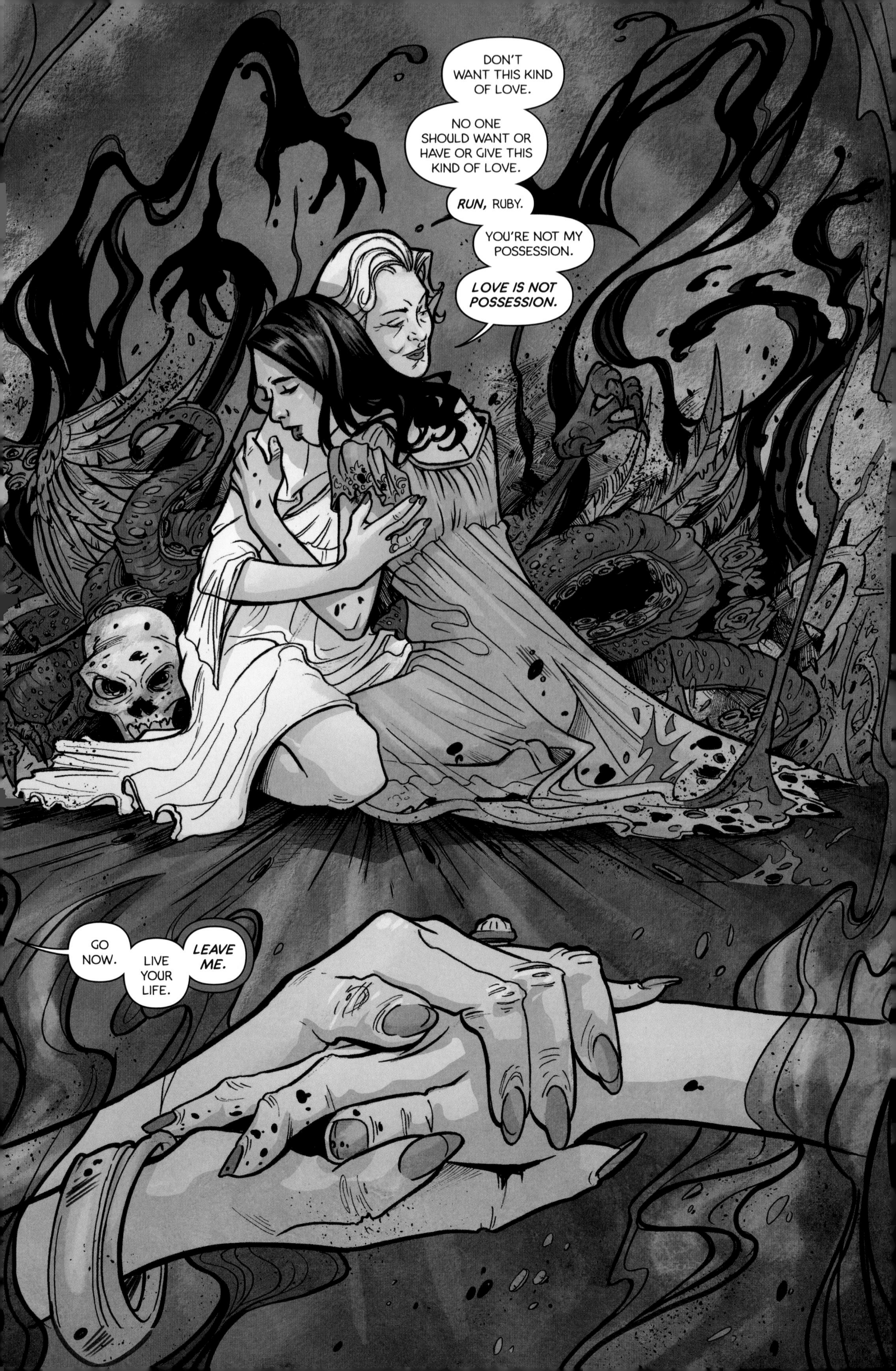
DON'T WANT THIS KIND OF LOVE.
NO ONE SHOULD WANT OR HAVE OR GIVE THIS KIND OF LOVE.
RUN, RUBY.
YOU'RE NOT MY POSSESSION.
LOVE IS NOT POSSESSION.
GO NOW.
LIVE YOUR LIFE.
LEAVE ME.

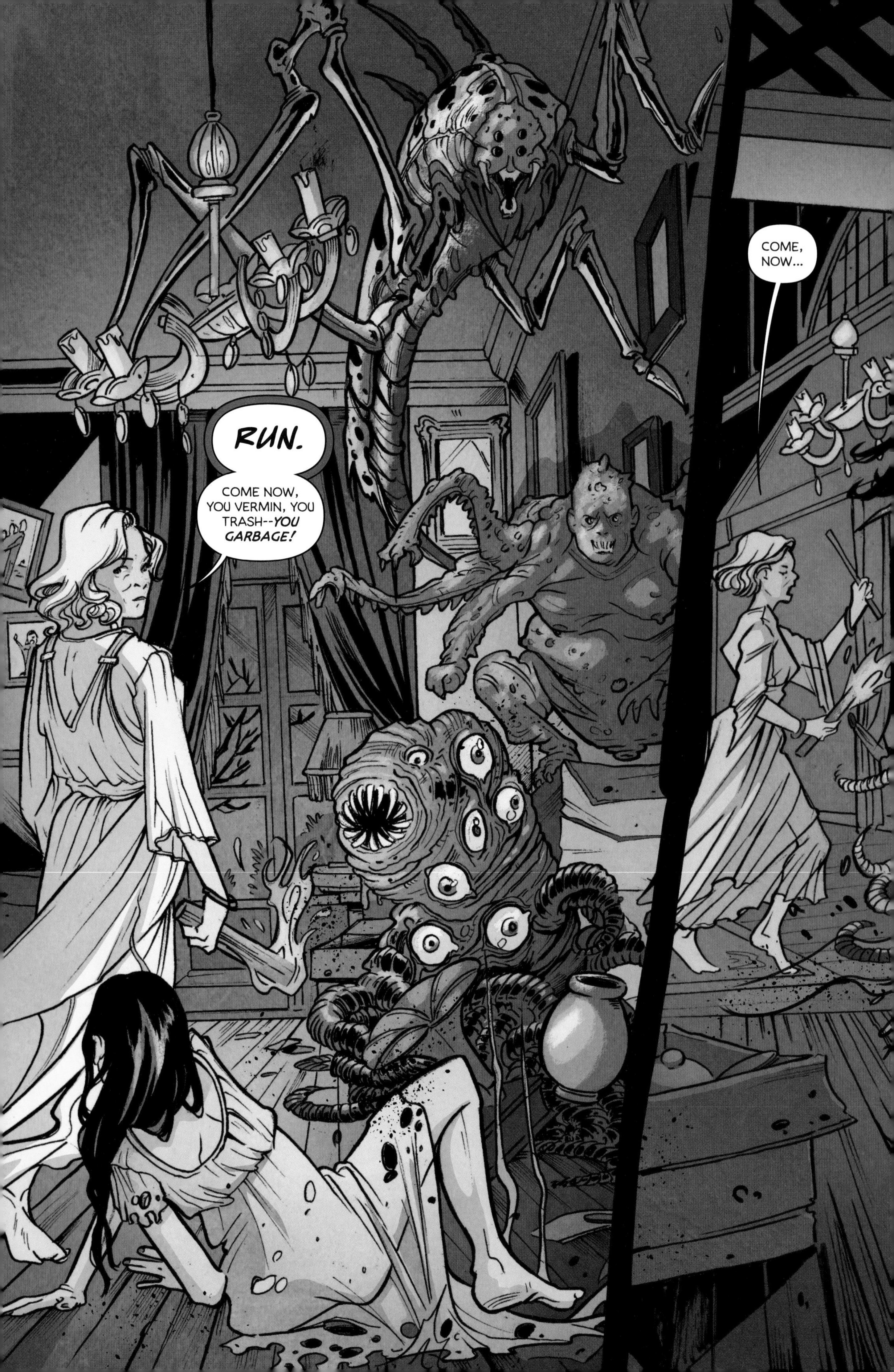
RUN.
COME NOW, YOU VERMIN, YOU TRASH--YOU GARBAGE!
COME, NOW...

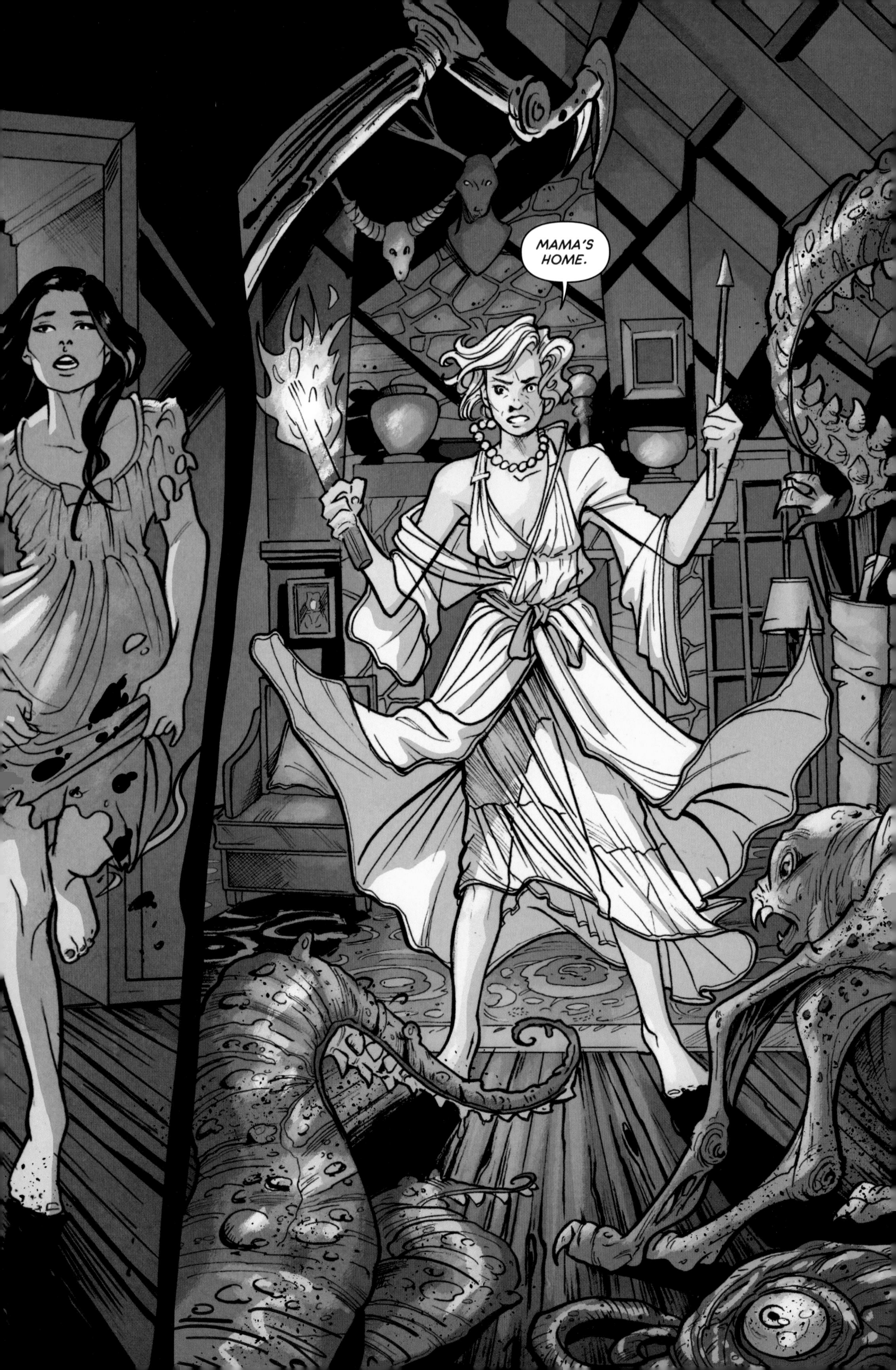
MAMA'S HOME.

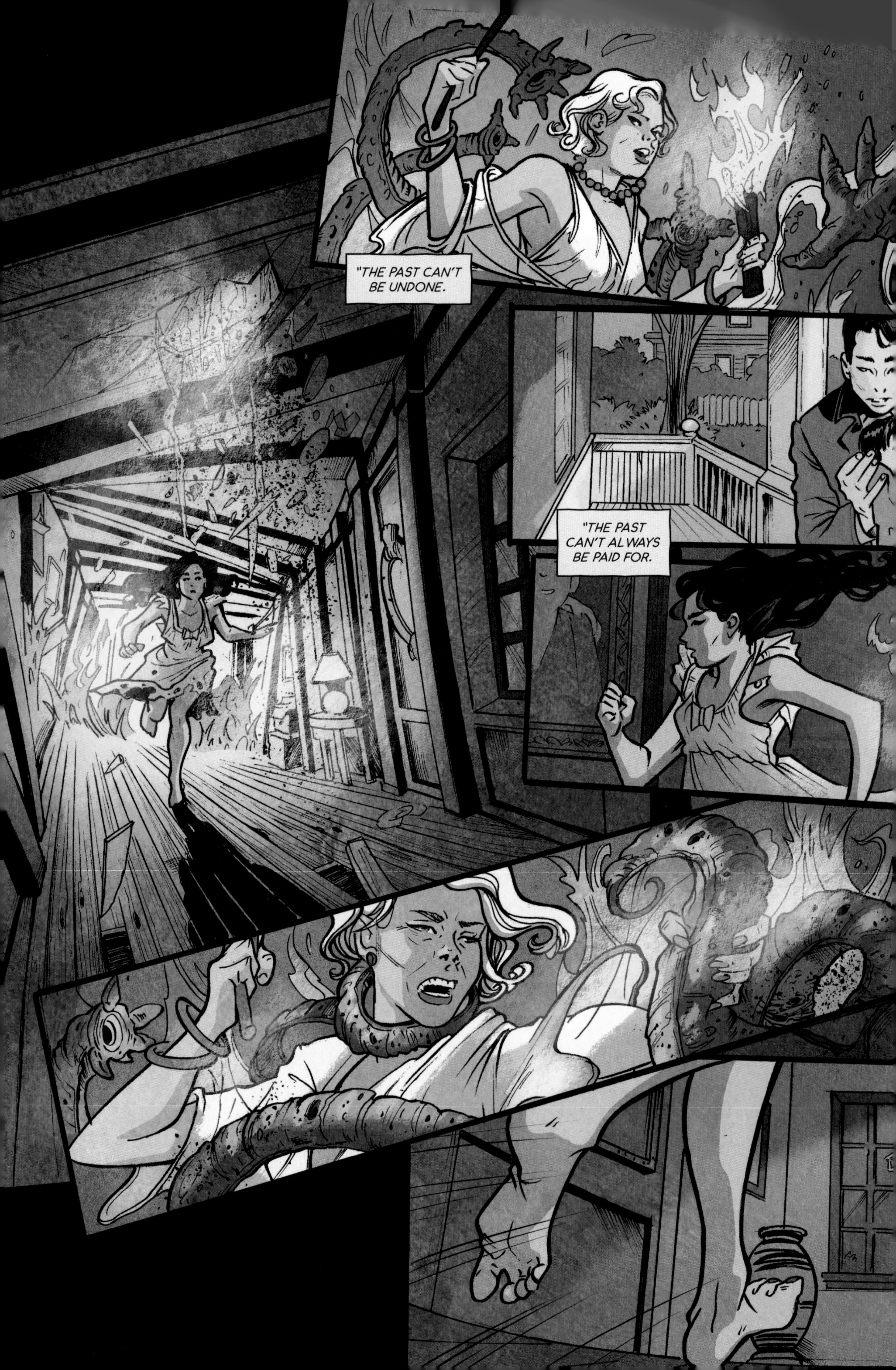
"THE PAST CAN'T
BE UNDONE.
"THE PAST
CAN'T ALWAYS
BE PAID FOR.

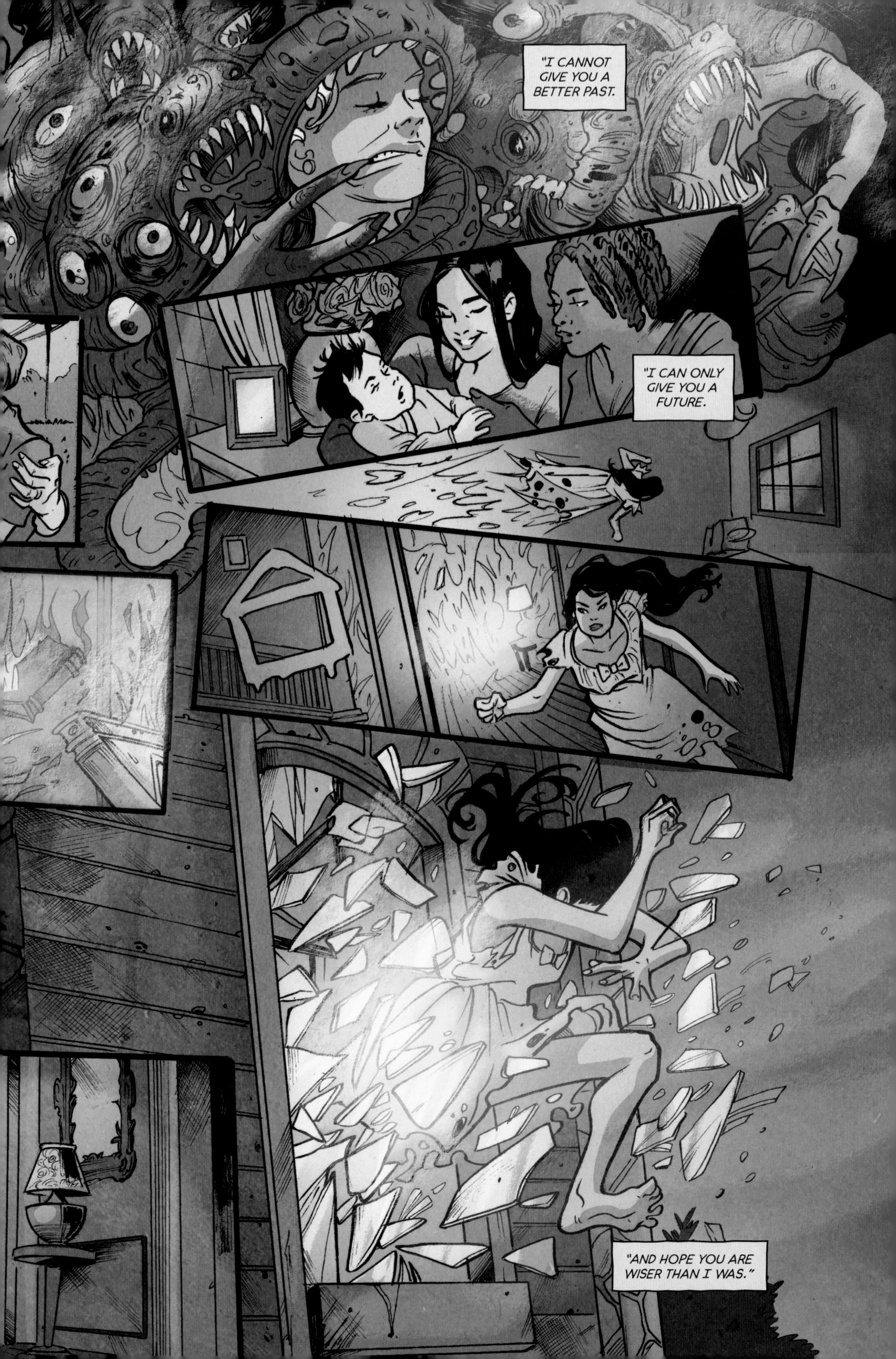
"I CANNOT GIVE YOU A BETTER PAST.
"I CAN ONLY GIVE YOU A FUTURE.
"AND HOPE YOU ARE WISER THAN I WAS."

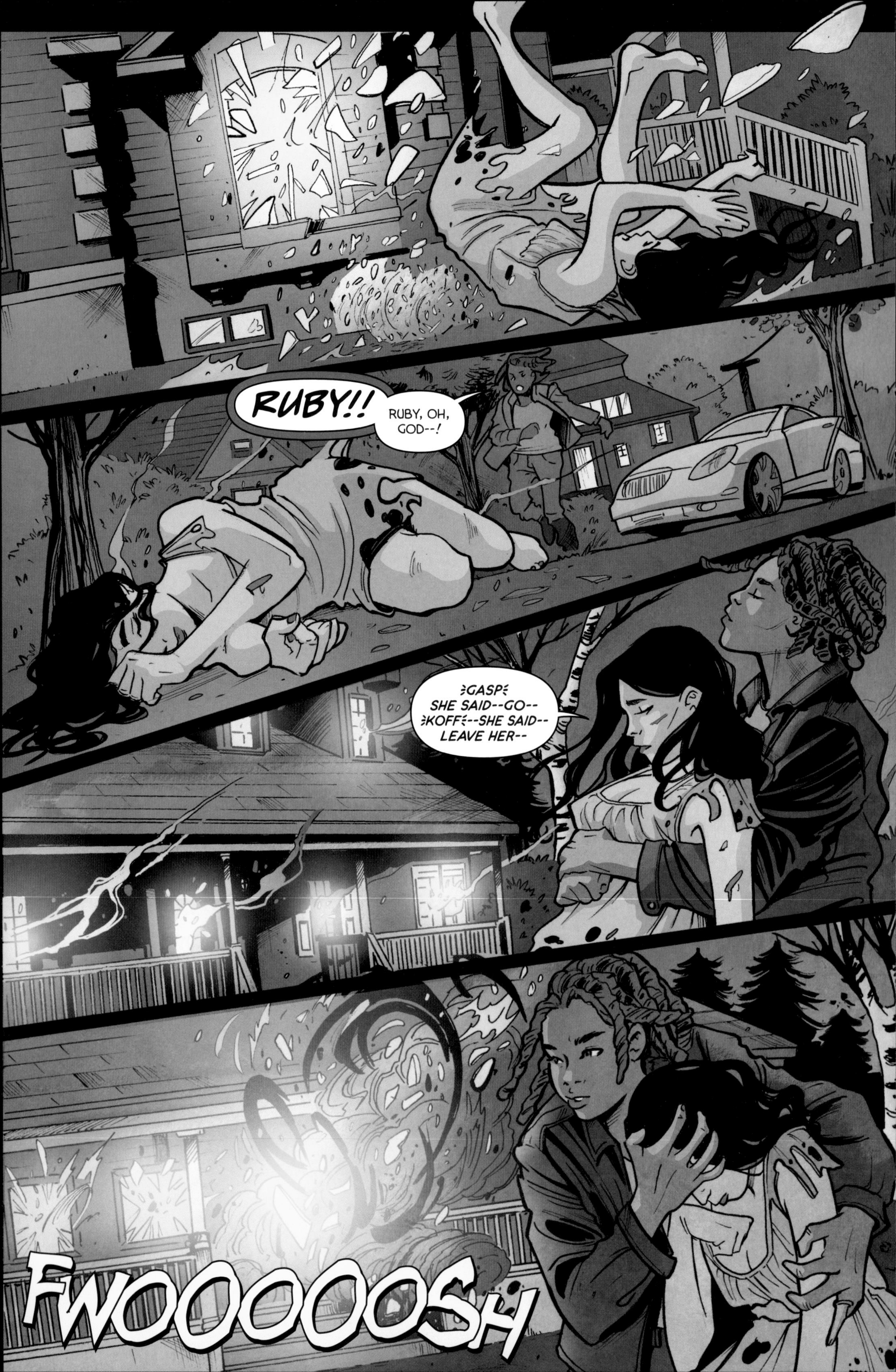
RUBY!!
RUBY, OH, GOD--!
GASP SHE SAID--GO-- KOFF--SHE SAID-- LEAVE HER--
FWOOOOOSH

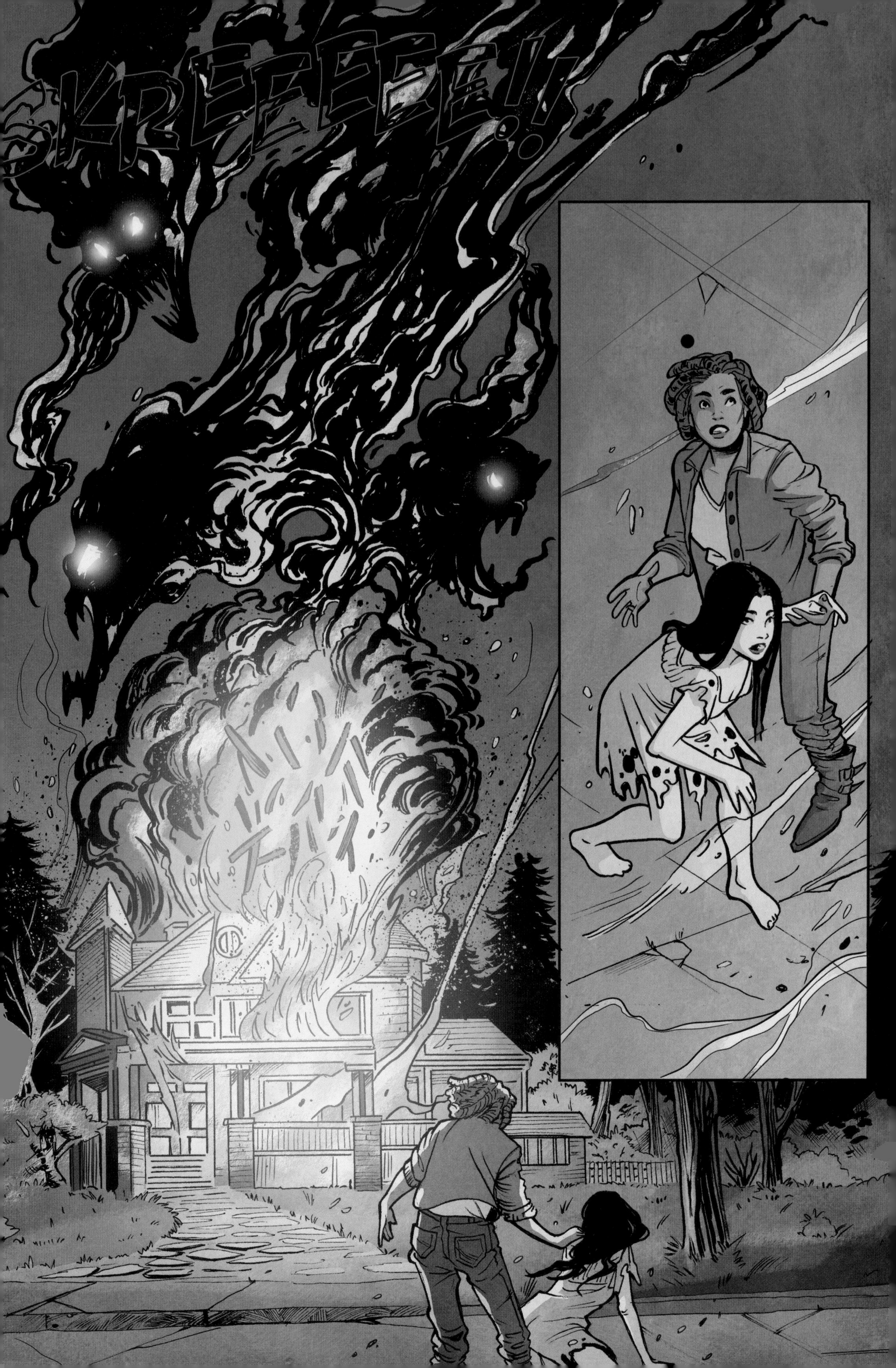
SKREEEEE!!

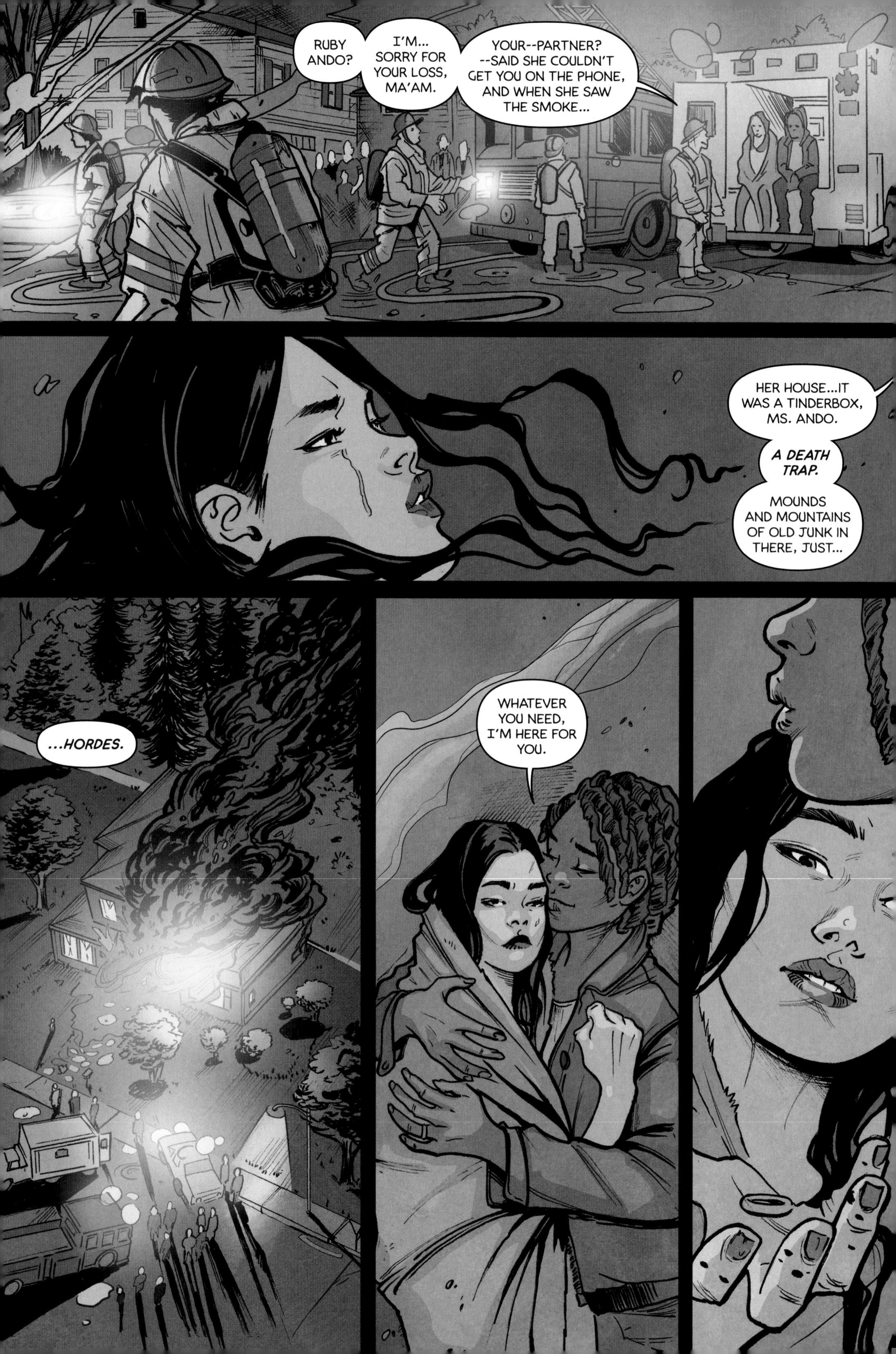
RUBY ANDO?
I'M... SORRY FOR YOUR LOSS, MA'AM.
YOUR--PARTNER? --SAID SHE COULDN'T GET YOU ON THE PHONE, AND WHEN SHE SAW THE SMOKE...
HER HOUSE...IT WAS A TINDERBOX, MS. ANDO.
A DEATH TRAP.
MOUNDS AND MOUNTAINS OF OLD JUNK IN THERE, JUST...
...HORDES.
WHATEVER YOU NEED, I'M HERE FOR YOU.

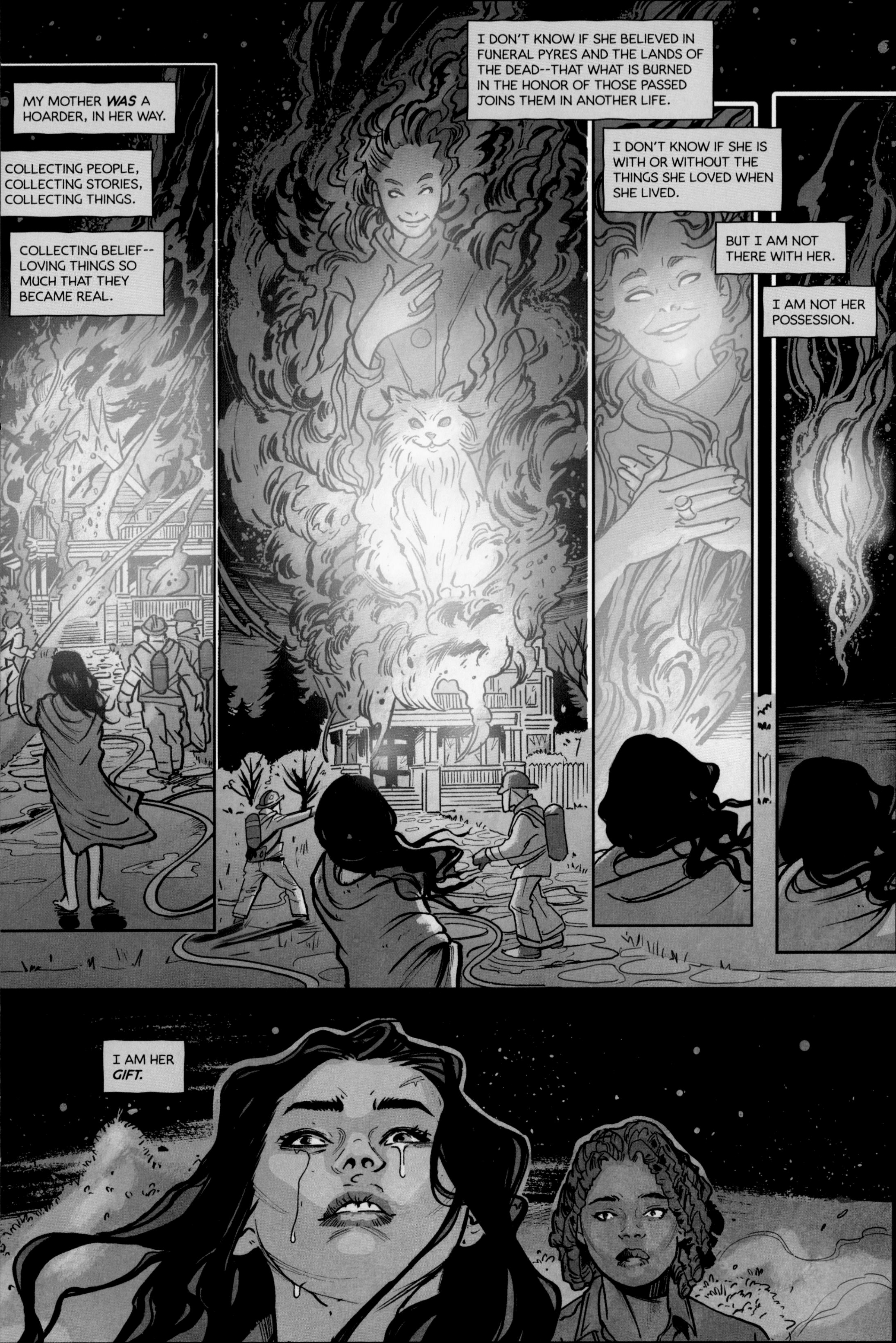
MY MOTHER *WAS* A HOARDER, IN HER WAY.
COLLECTING PEOPLE, COLLECTING STORIES, COLLECTING THINGS.
COLLECTING BELIEF-- LOVING THINGS SO MUCH THAT THEY BECAME REAL.
I DON'T KNOW IF SHE BELIEVED IN FUNERAL PYRES AND THE LANDS OF THE DEAD--THAT WHAT IS BURNED IN THE HONOR OF THOSE PASSED JOINS THEM IN ANOTHER LIFE.
I DON'T KNOW IF SHE IS WITH OR WITHOUT THE THINGS SHE LOVED WHEN SHE LIVED.
BUT I AM NOT THERE WITH HER.
I AM NOT HER POSSESSION.
I AM HER *GIFT.*

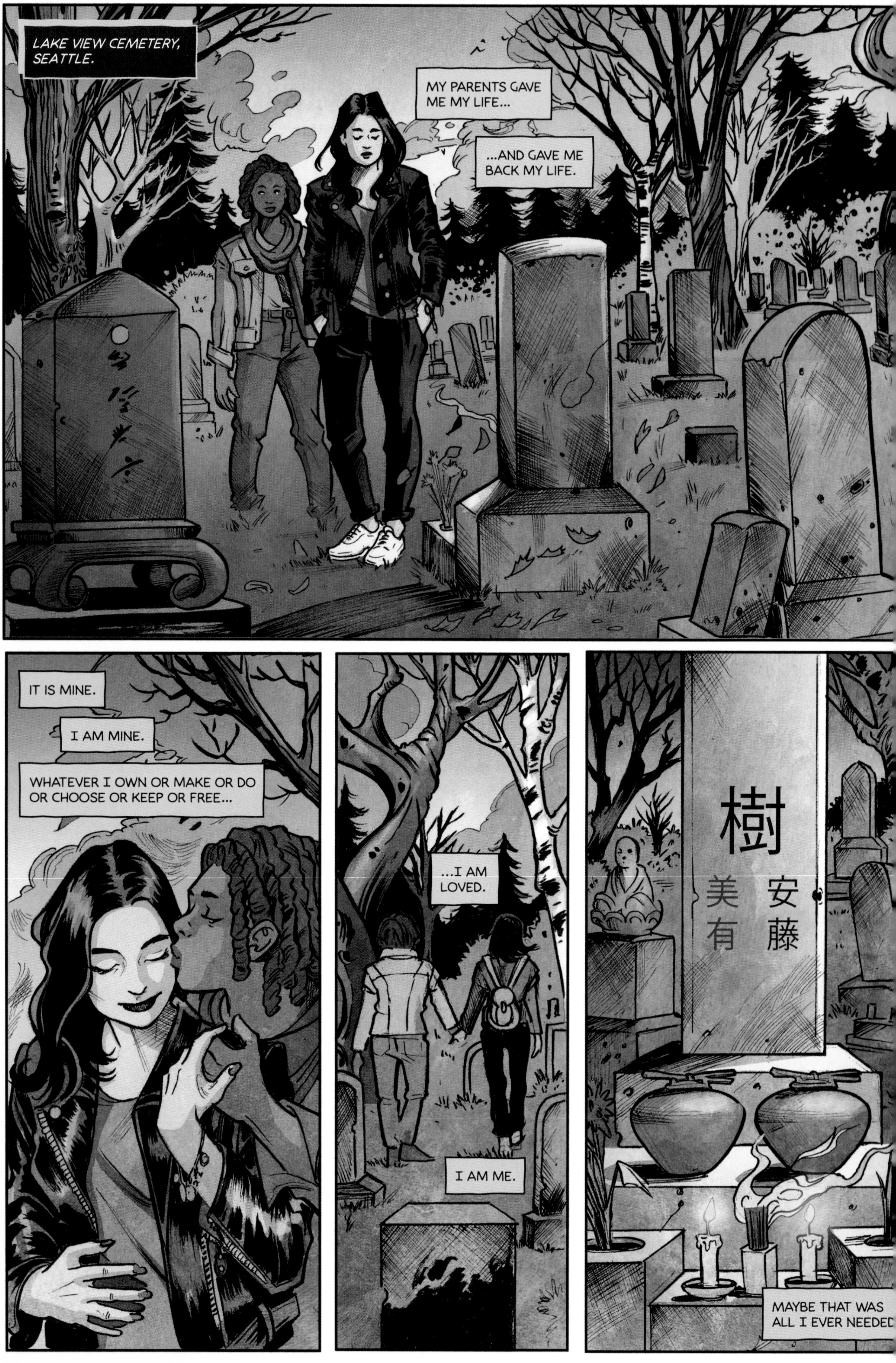
LAKE VIEW CEMETERY, SEATTLE.
MY PARENTS GAVE ME MY LIFE...
...AND GAVE ME BACK MY LIFE.
IT IS MINE.
I AM MINE.
WHATEVER I OWN OR MAKE OR DO OR CHOOSE OR KEEP OR FREE...
...I AM LOVED.
I AM ME.
樹
安藤
美有
MAYBE THAT WAS ALL I EVER NEEDED

BOUT THE CREATORS OF

HORDE™

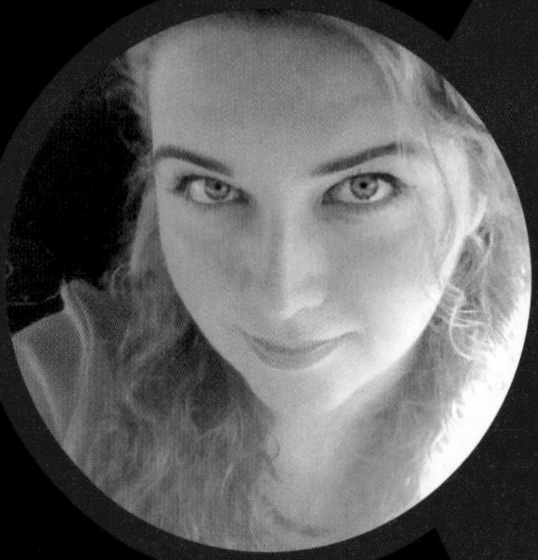

MARGUERITE BENNETT writer

@EvilMarguerite

Marguerite Bennett is a comic book writer from Richmond, Virginia, who currently splits her time between Los Angeles and New York City. She received her MFA in Creative Writing from Sarah Lawrence College in 2013 and quickly went on to work for DC Comics, Marvel, BOOM! Studios, Dynamite, and IDW on projects ranging from *Batman, Bombshells,* and *A-Force* to *Angela: Asgard's Assassin, Red Sonja,* and FOX TV's *Sleepy Hollow*.

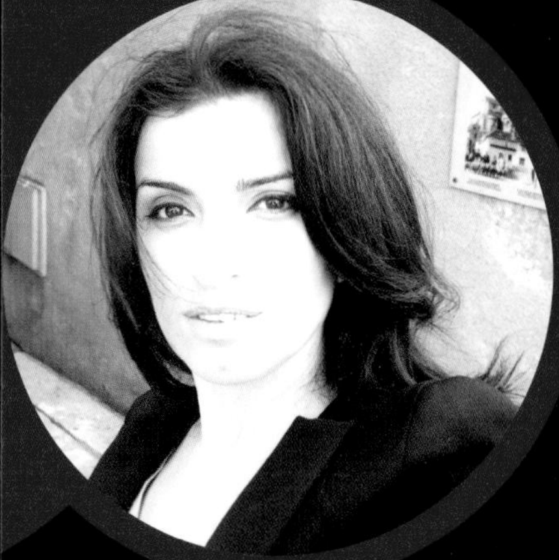

LEILA LEIZ artist

@LeilaLeiz

Born and raised in Italy, Leila is a self-taught artist who has seen her lifelong dream of working in American comics come true. After working for several years at European publishers like Soleil and Sergio Bonelli, Leila made the exciting jump to AfterShock Comics, where she began her new adventure on Paul Jenkins' series ALTERS, and continues the adventure with HORDE.

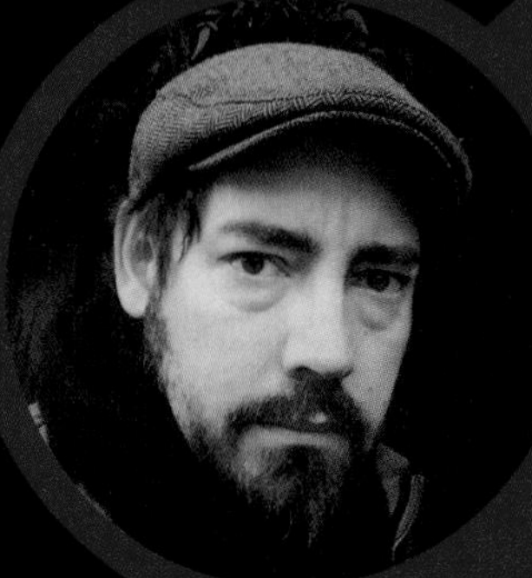

GUY MAJOR colorist

@GuyMajor

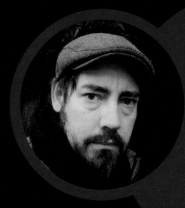

Guy Major is an artist and photographer who has been working in comics since 1995, when he responded to an ad looking for colorists for Wildstorm's *WildC.A.T.S.* series. He worked for Homage Studios until 1998 when he became a freelance color artist. He has worked on just about every character from Batman to Barry Ween. When not working on comics or out with his camera, he is studying about, tasting or drinking wine. He currently lives in Oakland, CA with two amazing women—his wife Jackie and their daughter Riley.

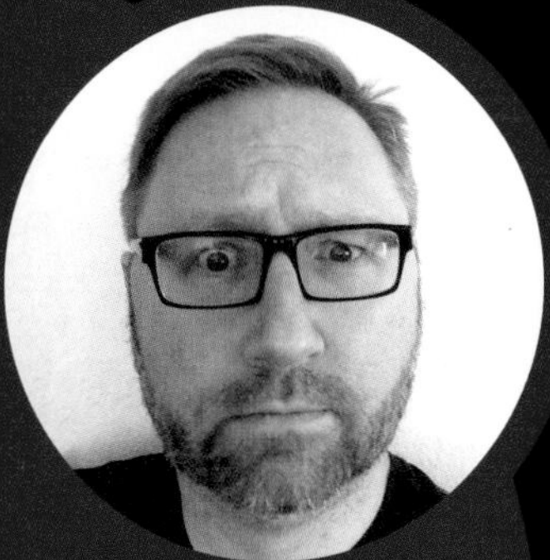

MARSHALL DILLON letterer

@MarshallDillon

A comic book industry veteran, Marshall got his start in 1994, in the midst of the indy comic boom. Over the years, he's been everything from an independent self-published writer to an associate publisher working on properties like G.I. Joe, Voltron and Street Fighter. He's done just about everything except draw a comic book, and has worked for just about every publisher except the "big two." Primarily a father and letterer these days, he also dabbles in old-school paper & dice RPG game design. You can catch up with Marshall at firstdraftpress.net.

STOCK UP ON THESE GREAT AFTERSHOCK
COLLECTIONS!

A WALK THROUGH HELL VOL 1
GARTH ENNIS / GORAN SUDZUKA
SEP181388, ON SALE 11/18

ALTERS VOL 1 & VOL 2
PAUL JENKINS / LEILA LEIZ
MAR171244 & APR181239

AMERICAN MONSTER VOL 1
BRIAN AZZARELLO / JUAN DOE
SEP161213

ANIMOSITY YEAR ONE, VOL 1, VOL 2 & VOL 3
MARGUERITE BENNETT / RAFAEL DE LATORRE
FEB181034, JAN171219, AUG171130 & MAY181314

ANIMOSITY: EVOLUTION VOL 1 & VOL 2
MARGUERITE BENNETT / ERIC GAPSTUR
MAR181079 & FEB188089

ANIMOSITY: THE RISE HARDCOVER
MARGUERITE BENNETT / JUAN DOE
AUG178324

ART OF JIM STARLIN HARDCOVER
JIM STARLIN
MAR181077

BABYTEETH YEAR ONE, VOL 1 & VOL 2
DONNY CATES / GARRY BROWN
OCT181328, OCT171087 & APR181225

BETROTHED VOL 1
SEAN LEWIS / STEVE UY
ON SALE 2/19

BLACK-EYED KIDS VOL 1, VOL 2 & VOL 3
JOE PRUETT / SZYMON KUDRANSKI
AUG161115, FEB171100 & JAN181152

BROTHERS DRACUL VOL 1
CULLEN BUNN / MIRKO COLAK
SEP181404

CAPTAIN KID VOL 1
MARK WAID / TOM PEYER / WILFREDO TORRES
APR171231

COLD WAR VOL 1
CHRISTOPHER SEBELA / HAYDEN SHERMAN
JUL181518

DARK ARK VOL 1 & VOL 2
CULLEN BUNN / JUAN DOE
FEB181035 & SEP181394

DREAMING EAGLES HARDCOVER
GARTH ENNIS / SIMON COLEBY
AUG161114

ELEANOR & THE EGRET VOL 1
JOHN LAYMAN / SAM KIETH
DEC171041

FU JITSU VOL 1
JAI NITZ / WESLEY ST. CLAIRE
APR181241

HER INFERNAL DESCENT VOL 1
LONNIE NADLER / ZAC THOMPSON / KYLE CHARLES / EOIN MARRION
OCT181341

HOT LUNCH SPECIAL VOL 1
ELIOT RAHAL / JORGE FORNES
ON SALE 2/19

INSEXTS YEAR ONE, VOL 1 & VOL 2
MARGUERITE BENNETT / ARIELA KRISTANTINA
APR181228, JUN161072 & SEP171098

JIMMY'S BASTARDS VOL & VOL 2
GARTH ENNIS / RUSS BRAUN
DEC171040 & JUN181333

MONSTRO MECHANICA VOL 1
PAUL ALLOR / CHRIS EVENHUIS
JUL181517

PESTILENCE VOL 1 & VOL 2
FRANK TIERI / OLEG OKUNEV
NOV171154, OCT181340

RELAY VOL 1
ZAC THOMPSON / ANDY CLARKE / RYAN BODENHEIM
ON SALE 1/19

ROUGH RIDERS VOL 1, VOL 2 & VOL 3
ADAM GLASS / PATRICK OLLIFFE
OCT161101, SEP171097 & AUG181474

SECOND SIGHT VOL 1
DAVID HINE / ALBERTO PONTICELL
DEC161186

SHIPWRECK VOL 1
WARREN ELLIS / PHIL HESTER
MAR181078

SHOCK HARDCOVER
VARIOUS
MAY161029

SUPERZERO VOL 1
AMANDA CONNER / JIMMY PALMIOTTI / RAFAEL DE LAT
MAY161029

THE LOST CITY EXPLORERS VO
ZACHARY KAPLAN / ALVARO SARRASECA
ON SALE 1/19

THE NORMALS VOL 1
ADAM GLASS / DENNIS CALERO
SEP181391

UNHOLY GRAIL VOL 1
CULLEN BUNN / MIRKO COLAK
JAN181151

WITCH HAMMER OGN
CULLEN BUNN / DALIBOR TALAJIC
SEP181387

WORLD READER VOL 1
JEFF LOVENESS / JUAN DOE
SEP171096

www.aftershockcomics.com/collections